W. E. (William Ewart) Gladstone

The Church of England and ritualism

W. E. (William Ewart) Gladstone

The Church of England and ritualism

ISBN/EAN: 9783337334246

Printed in Europe, USA, Canada, Australia, Japan

Cover: Foto ©Lupo / pixelio.de

More available books at **www.hansebooks.com**

THE CHURCH OF ENGLAND AND RITUALISM.

BY THE

RIGHT HON. W. E. GLADSTONE, M.P.

Reprinted from "The Contemporary Review," and revised.

ἀμέραι δ' ἐπίλοιποι
μάρτυρες σοφώτατοι.
PINDAR.

STRAHAN & CO., PUBLISHERS,
34, PATERNOSTER ROW, LONDON.

ADVERTISEMENT.

To this reprint of two articles from the *Contemporary Review*, on subjects which have much disturbed the Church of England, I prefix an observation on a single point, that of attaching doctrinal significance to external usages.

I have nowhere questioned that there are outward usages, which may and must be of doctrinal significance. My proposition is simply this, that where external usages have become subjects of contention, and that contention is carried to issue in courts of law, the field should not be unnecessarily widened; and the usage should not be interpreted for judicial purposes with reference to this or that particular dogma, so long, and of course only so long, as it naturally and unconstrainedly bears (p. 51) some sense not curtailing such a consequence.

Within the last few weeks has been taken from amongst us the venerated Dean Hook, the greatest parish priest of his age. I believe he had taken his part, in a decided and public manner, against the prohibition of the eastward position of the consecrator in the celebration of the Lord's Supper.

ADVERTISEMENT.

I am glad to have an opportunity of showing, as I think conclusively, how little it was in his mind hereby to exclude the laity from their full participation in the solemn act, by citing a passage from a private letter which he addressed to a young clergyman in 1842, when questions of outward usage were debated among us with what all *now* see to have been a needless heat and violence. "I am afraid that many in their zeal for the Church forget Christ, and in maintaining the rights of the Clergy forget the rights of the laity; who are, as well as the Clergy, priests unto the Most High God, and who indeed have as large a portion of the Sacrifice of Prayer and Praise assigned to them in the Prayer-Book as the Clergy."

I seek to show, by this extract, how innocent must have been, in the mind of this admirable man, the usage of the eastward position, and how unwise and unjust it would have been, in his case among others, to attach to it the 'doctrinal significance' of an intention to exclude the laity from their share in the Eucharistic offering.

I believe it may be stated with confidence that there have been times, when the northward position has been recommended, with authority and learning, as being *more* adapted than the eastward one to give full effect to the teaching of the Sacrifice in the Lord's Supper.

The notes appended to this reprint are in brackets.

W. E. G.

12th *November*, 1875.

RITUAL AND RITUALISM.*

For some months past, and particularly during the closing weeks of the Session of Parliament, the word Ritualism has had, in a remarkable degree, possession of the public ear, and of the public mind. So much is clear. The road is not so easy, when we proceed to search for the exact meaning of the term. And yet the term itself is not in fault. It admits, at first sight, of an easy and unexceptionable definition. Ritualism surely means an undue disposition to ritual. Ritual itself is founded on the Apostolic precept, "Let all things be done decently and in order;" $εὐσχημόνως$ $καὶ$ $κατὰ$ $τάξιν$, in right, graceful, or becoming figure, and by fore-ordered arrangement, 1 Cor. xiv. 40. The exterior modes of divine service are thus laid down as a distinct and proper subject for the consideration of Christians.

But the word Ritualism passes in the public mind

* From *The Contemporary Review* for October, 1874.

for something more specific in terms, and also for something more variable, if not more vague, in character. In a more specific form it signifies such a kind and such a manner of undue disposition to ritual as indicate a design to alter at least the ceremonial of religion established in and by this nation, for the purpose of assimilating it to the Roman or Popish ceremonial; and, further, of introducing the Roman or Papal religion into this country, under the insidious form, and silent but steady suasion, of its ceremonial.

All this is intelligible enough; and, if we start with such a conception of Ritualism, we, as a people, ought to know what we think, say, and do about it. But there is another and a briefer account which may be given of it. There is a definition purely subjective, but in practice more widely prevalent than any other. According to this definition, Ritualism is to each man that which, in matter of ritual, each man dislikes, and holds to be in excess. When the term is thus used, it becomes in the highest degree deceptive; for it covers under an apparent unity meanings as many as the ripples of the smiling sea; as the shades of antagonism to, or divergence from, the most overloaded Roman ceremonial. When the term is thus employed, sympathy flies, as if it were electricity, through the crowd; but it is sympathy based upon the sound and not upon the sense. Men thus impelled mischievously but naturally mistake the strength of their feeling for the strength of their argument. The heated mind resents the chill touch and relentless scrutiny of logic. There could be no advantage, especially at the present time, in approaching such a theme from this point of view.

But perhaps it may be allowable to make an endeavour to carry this subject for a few moments out of the polemical field into the domain of thought. I have but little faith in coercion applied to matter of opinion and feeling, let its titles be ever so clear. But a word spoken in quietness, and by way of appeal to the free judgment and reason of men, can rarely fail to be in season. I propose, accordingly, to consider what is the true measure and meaning of Ritual, in order thus to arrive at a clear conception of that vice in its use which is designated by the name of Ritualism.

Ritual, then, is the clothing which, in some form, and in some degree, men naturally and inevitably give to the performance of the public duties of religion. Beyond the religious sphere the phrase is never carried; but the thing appears, and cannot but appear, under other names. In all the more solemn and stated public acts of man, we find employed that investiture of the acts themselves with an appropriate exterior, which is the essential idea of ritual. The subject-matter is different, but the principle is the same: it is the use and adaptation of the outward for the expression of the inward.

It may be asked, Why should there be any such adaptation? Why not leave things to take their course? Is not the inward enough, if it be genuine and pure? And may not the outward overlay and smother it? But human nature itself, with a thousand tongues, utters the reply. The marriage of the outward and the inward pervades the universe.

> They wedded form with artful strife,
> The strength and harmony of life.

And the life and teaching of Christ Himself are marked by a frequent employment of signs in which are laid the ground, and the foreshowing, both of Sacraments and of Ritual.

True indeed it is that the fire, meant to warm, may burn us; the light, meant to guide, may blind us; the food, meant to sustain, may poison us; but fire and light and food are not only useful, they are indispensable. And so it is with that universal and perpetual instinct of human nature which exacts of us, that the form given externally to our thoughts in word and act shall be one appropriate to their substance. Applied to the circle of civilized life, this principle, which gives us ritual in religion, gives us the ceremonial of Courts, the costume of Judges, the uniform of regiments, all the language of heraldry and symbol, all the hierarchy of rank and title; and which, descending through all classes, presents itself in the badges and the bands of Foresters' and Shepherds' Clubs and Benefit Societies.

But if there be a marriage—ordained by Providence and pervading Nature—of the outward and the inward, it is required in this, as in other marriages, that there be some harmony of disposition between the partners. In the perception of this harmony, a life-long observation has impressed me with the belief that we as a people are, as a rule, and apart from special training, singularly deficient. In the inward realms of thought and of imagination, the title of England to stand in the first rank of civilized nations need not be argued, for it is admitted. It would be equally idle to offer any special plea on its behalf in reference to all classes of developments purely external. The railway and the telegraph, the factory, the forge, and the mine; the highways beaten upon every ocean; the first place in the trade of the world, where population would give us but the fifth; a commercial marine equalling that of the whole of Continental Europe: these may be left to tell their own tale. When we come to pure Art, we find ourselves beaten by great countries, and even, in one case at least, by small.* But it is not of pure Art that I would now speak. It is of that vast and diversified region of human life and action, where a distinct purpose of utility is pursued, and where the instrument employed aspires at the same time to an outward form of beauty. Here lies the great mass and substance of the *Kunst-leben*—the Art-life, of a people. Its sphere is so large, that nothing except pure thought is of right excluded from it. As in the Italian language scarcely a word can be found which is not musical, so a music of the eye (I borrow the figure from Wordsworth) should pervade all visible production and construction whatever, whether of objects in themselves permanent, or of those where a temporary collocation only of the parts is in view. This state of things was realized, to a great extent, in the Italian life of the middle ages. But its grand and normal example is to be sought in ancient Greece, where the spirit of Beauty was so profusely poured forth, that it seemed to fill the life and action of

* Belgium.

man as it fills the kingdoms of Nature: the one, like the other, was in its way a *Kosmos*. The elements of production, everything embodied under the hand or thought of man, fell spontaneously into beautiful form, like the glasses in a kaleidoscope. It was the gallant endeavour to give beauty as a matter of course, and in full harmony with purpose, to all that he manufactured and sold, which has made the name of Wedgwood now, and I trust for ever, famous. The Greeks, at least the Attic Greeks, were, so to speak, a nation of Wedgwoods. Most objects, among those which we produce, we calmly and without a sigh surrender to Ugliness, as if we were coolly passing our children through the fire to Moloch. But in Athens, as we know from the numberless relics of Greek art and industry in every form, the production of anything ugly would have startled men by its strangeness as much as it would have vexed them by its deformity; and a deviation from the law of Taste, the faculty by which Beauty is discerned, would have been treated simply as a deviation from the law of Nature. One and the same principle, it need hardly be observed, applies to material objects which are produced once for all, and to matters in which, though the parts may subsist before and after, the combination of them is for the moment only. The law that governed the design of an amphora or a lamp, governed also the order of a spectacle, a procession, or a ceremonial. It was not the sacrifice of the inward meaning to the outward show: that method of proceeding was a glorious discovery reserved for the later, and especially for our own, time. Neither was it the sacrifice even of the outward to the inward. The Greek did not find it requisite: Nature had not imposed upon him such a necessity. It was the determination of their meeting-point; the expression of the harmony between the two. It is in regard to the perception and observance of this law that the English, nay, the British people, ought probably to be placed last among the civilized nations of Europe.' And if it be so, the first thing is to bring into existence and into activity a real consciousness of the defect. We need not, if it exist, set it down to natural and therefore incurable inaptitude. It is more probably due to the disproportionate application of our given store of faculties in other directions. To a great extent it may be true that for the worship of beauty we have substituted a successful pursuit of comfort. But are the two in conflict? And first of all, is the charge against us, as we are, a just one?

To make good imputations of any kind against

ourselves is but an invidious office. It would be more agreeable to leave the trial to the impartial reflection and judgment of each man. But one of the features of the case is this, that so few among us have taken the pains to form, in such matters, even a habit of observation. And, again, there are certain cases of exception to the general rule. For example, take the instance of our rural habitations. I do not speak of their architecture, nor especially do I speak of our more pretentious dwellings. But the English garden is proverbial for beauty; and the English cottage garden stands almost alone in the world. Except where smoke, stench, and the havoc of manufacturing and mining operations have utterly deformed the blessed face of Nature, the English cottager commonly and spontaneously provides some little pasture for his eye by clothing his home in the beauty of shrubs and flowers. And even where he has been thus violently deprived of his lifelong communion with Nature, or where his lot is cast in huge cities from which he scarcely ever escapes, he still resorts to potted flowers and to the song of caged birds for solace. This love of natural objects, which are scarcely ever without beauty or grace, ought to supply a basis on which to build all that is still wanting. But I turn to another chapter. The ancient ecclesiastical architecture of this country indicates a more copiously diffused love and pursuit of beauty, and a richer faculty for its production, in connection with purpose, than is to be found in the churches of any other part of Christendom. Not that we possess in our cathedrals and greater edifices the most splendid of all examples. But the parish churches of England are as a whole unrivalled; and it has been the opinion of persons of the widest knowledge, that they might even challenge without fear the united parish churches of Europe, from their wealth of beauty in all the particulars of their own styles of architecture.

Still, it does not appear that these exceptions impair the force of the general proposition, which is that as a people we are, in the business of combining beauty with utility, singularly uninstructed, unaccomplished, maladroit, unhandy. If instances must be cited, they are not far to seek. Consider the unrivalled ugliness of our towns in general. Or put Englishmen to march in a procession, and see how, instead of feeling instinctively the music and sympathy of motion, they will loll, and stroll, and straggle; it never occurs to them that there is beauty or solemnity in ordered movement, and that the instruction required is only that simple instruction which, without speech, Nature should herself supply to her pupils.

<blockquote>Quid facerent, ipsi nullo didicere magistro.</blockquote>

Take again—sad as it is to strike for once at the softer portion of the species—the dress of Englishwomen, which, apart from rank and special gift or training or opportunity, is reputed to be the worst in the European world, and the most wanting alike in character and in adaptation. Take the degraded state, in point of beauty, at which all the arts of design, and all industrial production, had arrived among us some fifty years ago, in the iron age of George IV., and before the reaction which has redeemed many of them from disgrace, and raised some to real excellence.

But, indeed, in too many cases, our repentance is almost worse than our transgressions. When we begin to imbibe the conception that, after all, there is no reason why attempts should not be made to associate Beauty with usefulness, the manner of our attempts is too frequently open to the severest criticism. The so-called Beauty is administered in portentous doses of ornamentation sometimes running to actual deformity. Quantity is the measure, not quality, nor proportion. Who shall now compete with the awakened Englishwoman for the house of hair built upon her head, or for the measureless extension of her draggling train? Who shall be the rival of some English architects plastering their work with an infinity of pretentious detail in order to screen from attention inharmonious dimension and poverty of lines? Or—that I may without disguise direct the charge against the mind and spirit of the nation, embodied in its Parliament and its Government— what age or country can match the practical solecisms exhibited in the following facts and others like them? Forty years ago we determined to erect the most extensive building of Pointed architecture in the world; namely, our Houses of Parliament, or, as they are called, the Palace of Westminster. We entrusted the work to our most eminent Italian architect. Once was pretty well; but once was not enough. So, twenty years ago, we determined to erect another vast building in the Italian style; namely, a pile of public offices, or, as some would call it, a Palace of Administration; and we committed the erection of it to our most experienced and famous architect in the Pointed species. Thus each man was selected for his unacquaintance with the genius of the method in which he was to work. Who can wonder, in circumstances like these, that the spirit and soul of style are so often forgotten in its letter; that beauty itself unlearns itself, and degenerates into mere display; that for the attainment of a given end, not economy of means, but profusion of means, becomes our law and our boast; that, in the Houses of Parliament, dispersion of the essential parts over the widest possible space marks a building where the closest concentration should have been the rule; and that the Foreign Office, which is a workshop, exhibits a Staircase which no palace of the Sovereign can match in its dimensions?

If from the work of creation we turn to the world of action, the same incapacity of detecting discord, and the same tendency to solecism will appear. In what country except ours could (as I know to have happened) a parish ball have been got up in order to supply funds for procuring a parish hearse?

I shall not admit that, in these remarks, I have gone astray from the title and subject of the paper. What is Ritualism? It is unwise, undisciplined reaction from poverty, from coldness, from barrenness, from nakedness; it is overlaying Purpose with adventitious and obstructive incumbrance; it is departure from measure and from harmony in the annexation of appearance to substance, of the outward to the inward; it is the caricature of the Beautiful; it is the conversion of helps into hindrances; it is the attempted substitution of the secondary for the primary aim, and the real failure and paralysis of both. A great deal of our architecture, a great share of our industrial production has been or is, it may be feared, very Ritualistic indeed.

Let us now trace the operation of the same principle in the subject-matter of religion. We encounter the same defects, the same difficulties, the same excesses; the same want of trained habits of observation; the same forgetfulness of proportion; the same danger of burying it under a mass of ornament.

It must be admitted that the state of things, from which the thing popularly known as Ritualism took historically its point of departure, was dishonouring to Christianity, disgraceful to the nation; disgraceful most of all to that much-vaunted religious sentiment of the English public, which in impenetrable somnolence endured it, and resented all interference with it. Nakedness enough there was, fifty and forty years ago, of divine service and of religious edifices, among the Presbyterians of Scotland, and among the Nonconformists of England. But, among these, the outward fault was to a great extent redeemed by the cardinal virtues of earnestness and fervour. The prayer of the minister was at least listened to with a pious attention, and the noblest of all the sounds that can reach the human ear was usually heard in the massive swell, and solemn fall, of the united voices of the congregations. But within the ordinary English Parish Church of town or country, there was no such redeeming feature in the action of the living, though the inanimate treasure of the Prayer-book yet remained. Its warmth was stored, like the material of fire in our coal seams, for better days. It was still the surviving bed or mould, in which higher forms of religious thought and feeling were some day to be cast. But the actual state of things, as to worship, was bad beyond all parallel known to me in experience or reading. Taking together the expulsion of the poor and labouring classes (especially from the town churches), the mutilations and blockages of the fabrics, the baldness of the service, the elaborate horrors of the so-called music, with the jargon of parts contrived to exhibit the powers of every village roarer, and to prevent all congregational singing; and above all, the coldness and indifference of the lounging or sleeping congregations, our services were probably without a parallel in the world for their debasement; and as they would have shocked a Brahmin or a Buddhist, so they hardly could have been endured in this country had not the faculty of taste, and the perception of the seemly or unseemly, been as dead as the spirit of devotion.

There were exceptions, and the exceptions were beginning slowly to grow in number : but I speak of the general state of things, such as I can myself recollect it. In some places the older traditions and spirit of the Church had survived all the paralysing influences of the first Hanoverian generations ; in others they were commended to the people by the lofty spirit and English pluck of men like Dr. Hook; in many cathedrals, with stateliness, a remnant of true dignity was preserved; and in a third class of cases the clergy known as Evangelical had infused into their congregations a reverent sense of the purpose for which they met together. For this and other services they were pointed at with the finger of scorn by the very same stamp of people as those who are now most fervid in denouncing the opposite section. And it was for reasons not very different ; both were open to the charge that they did not thoroughly conform to the prescriptions of the Prayer-book; both were apt to slide into the attitude and feeling of a clique ; both rather abounded in self-confidence, and were viewed askance by authority ; both, it must be added, were zealous, and felt, or held, to be troublesome. But of the general tone of the services in the Church of England at that time I do not hesitate to say, it was such as when carefully considered would have shocked not only an earnest Christian of whatever communion, but any sincere believer in God, any one who held that there was a Creator and Governor of the world, and that His creatures ought to worship Him. And that which I wish to press upon the mind of the reader is, that this state of things was one with which the members of the Church generally were quite content. It was not by lay associations with long purses that the people were with difficulty and with much resistance awakened out of this state of things. It was by the reforming Bishops and Clergy of the Church of England. And, though the main source of the evil without doubt lay deeper, such an amount of effort could hardly have been needed, had the faculties and life of Art been more widely diffused in the country.

Had we, as a people, been possessed in reasonable measure of that sense of harmony between the inward and the outward, of which I have been lamenting the weakness, it could not indeed have supplied the place of a fervent religious life; but Divine worship, the great public symbol and pledge of that life, never could have fallen so low among us. And I think it has been in some measure from the same defect that, during the exterior revivals of the last forty years, there has been so much misapprehension and miscarriage, so much dissatisfaction and disturbance. More than thirty years have passed since agitation in London, and riot in Exeter, were resorted to for the purpose, as was conscientiously believed, of preserving the purity of the Reformed Religion against the use of the surplice in the pulpit, and of the Prayer for the Church Militant. In vain the bishops and the clergy concerned made their protests, and averred that they were advising, or acting, in simple "obedience to the law." The appeal to that watchword, now so sacred, was utterly unavailing: Popery, and nothing less than Popery, it was insisted, must be the meaning of these changes. To me it appeared at the time that their introduction, however legal, was, if not effected with the full and intelligent concurrence of the flocks, decidedly unwise. But as to these particular usages themselves, I held then, and hold now, that their tendency, when calmly viewed, must have been seen to be rather Protestant than Popish; that Popery would have led to the use of a different and lower garb in preaching, not to the use of the same vestment which was also to be used for the celebration of the Eucharist; and that no prayer in the Prayer-book bears so visibly the mark of the Reformation, as the Prayer for the Church Militant. Be that as it may, I recollect with pain a particular case, which may serve as a sample of the feeling, and the occurrences, of that day. An able and devoted young clergyman had accepted the charge of a new district parish in one of our largest towns, with trifling emoluments, and with large masses of neglected poor, whom he had begun steadily and successfully to gather in. Within a year or two an agitation was raised, not in his parish, but in the town at large; it had grown too hot to hold him; and he was morally compelled to retire from his benefice and from the place, for the offences of having preached the morning sermon in the surplice, read the Prayer for the Church Militant, and opened his church for Divine service, not daily, but on all festivals. The inference to be drawn from this is not an inference of self-laudation: not the ἡμεῖς τοι πατέρων μέγ' ἀμείνονες εὐχόμεθ' εἶναι·* but an inference in behalf of a little self-mistrust, and a great deal of deliberation and circumspection in these important matters. For, from a view of the modes which have become usual for the celebration of Divine service, in average churches not saddled with a party name, there appears this rather startling fact, that the congregations of the Church of England in general now practise without suspicion, and the Parliament, representing the general feeling out of doors, is disposed to enforce, by the establishment of more stringent procedure, what

* Il. iv. 405.

thirty years ago was denounced, and rather more than denounced, as Ritualism.

The truth is, that, in the word Ritualism, there is involved much more than the popular mind seems to suppose. The present movement in favour of ritual is not confined to ritualists, neither is it confined even to Churchmen. It has been, when all things are considered, quite as remarkable among Nonconformists and Presbyterians; not because they have as much of it, but because they formerly had none, and because their system appeared to have been devised and adjusted in order to prevent its introduction, and to fix upon it even *in limine* the aspect of a flagrant departure from first principles. Crosses on the outside of chapels, organs within them, rich painted architecture, that flagrant piece of symbolism, the steeple, windows filled with subjects in stained glass, elaborate chanting, the use of the Lord's prayer, which is no more than the thin end of the wedge that is to introduce fixed forms, and the partial movements in favour of such forms already developed, are among the signs which, taken all together, form a group of phenomena evidently referable to some cause far more deep and wide-working than mere servile imitation, or the fashion of the day. In the case of the organ, be it recollected that many who form part of the *crême de la crème* of Protestantism have now begun to use that which the Pope does not hear in his own Chapel or his sublime Basilica, and which the entire Eastern Church has ever shrunk from employing in its services.

With this I will mention a familiar matter, though it may provoke a smile. It is the matter of clerical costume; on which I will not scruple to say that, in my judgment, the party of costume is right. A costume for the clergy is as much connected with discipline and self-respect as an uniform for the army, and is no small guarantee for conduct. The disuse of clerical costume was a recent innovation; but thirty-five or forty years ago the abuse had become almost universal. It was consummated by the change in lay fashions—a very singular one—to a nearly exclusive use by men of black. The reaction began in the cut of the waistcoat, which, as worn by the innovators, was buttoned all the way up to the cravat. This was deemed so distinctly Popish, that it acquired the nickname of "The Mark of the Beast;" and it is a fact that, among the tailors of the west-end of London, this shape of waistcoat was familiarly known as "the M. B. waistcoat." Any one who will now take the pains to notice the dress of the regular Presbyterian or Dissenting minister will, I think, find that, in a great majority of instances, he too, when in his best, wears, like the clergyman, the M. B. waistcoat.

True the distance between these Presbyterian and Nonconforming services, and those of the Church of England, in point of ritual, remains as great, or perhaps greater, than before; but that is because one and the same forward movement has taken possession of both, only the speeds may have been different. I will give a case in point. Five and thirty years ago hardly any one had dreamt of a surpliced choir in a parish church. When such an use came in, it was thought to be like a sign of the double surperlative in High Churchmanship, and was deemed the most violent experiment yet made upon the patience of the laity. How stands the matter now? As the purity of Welsh Protestantism is well known, I will take an instance from Wales. In a Welsh town, of no great size, the clergyman of the parish was moved, not long ago, to introduce the surplice for his choir. He determined upon a *plébiscite*; and placed printed slips of paper about the seats, requesting a written aye or no. Near two hundred and fifty answers were given: and of the answers more than four-fifths were ayes.* In truth, there is a kind of ritual race; all have set their faces

* [Another case almost exactly similar has recently been reported in the newspapers at East Harborne, near Birmingham.]

the same way, and none like to have their relative backwardness enhanced, while the absolute standing-point is continually moved forward.

This is matter of fact, and of the very widest reach, compassing a field of which but a little corner was covered by the recent Act of Parliament; and now the question rises to the lip, Ought this matter of fact, which will scarcely be disputed, to be viewed with satisfaction or with displeasure?

In my opinion this is a question extremely difficult to answer; and I will not affect to be able to give it a complete reply. It seems to me that ritual is, in what amount I do not attempt now to inquire, a legitimate accompaniment, nay, effect, of the religious life; but I view with mistrust and jealousy all tendency, wherever shown, either to employ ritual as its substitute, or to treat ritual as its producing cause. All, however, that I have thus far endeavoured to insinuate is, that the subject is a very large one—that it cannot be dealt with offhand—that it is exceedingly significant and pregnant in the manifestations it supplies. If we do not live in one of the great thinking ages, we live in an age which supplies abundant materials of thought; and with the many problems, which we shall leave to our children for solution, we may hand down to them the cordial wish that they may make more profitable use of these materials than we have done.

If we survey the Christian world, we shall have occasion to observe that ritual does not bear an unvarying relation to doctrine. The most notable proof of this assertion is to be found in the Lutheran communion. It is strongly and, except where opinion has deviated in the direction of rationalism, uniformly Protestant. But in portions of the considerable area over which it stretches, for example, in Denmark, in Sweden and Norway, even on the inhospitable shores of Iceland, altars, vestments, lights, (if not even incense) are retained: the clergyman is called the priest, and the Communion Office is termed the Mass. But there is no distinction of doctrine whatever between Swedish or Danish, and German Lutherans: nor, according to the best authorities, has the chain of the Episcopal succession been maintained in those countries. Even in this country, there are some of those clergy who are called Broadchurchmen, some who have a marked indifference to doctrine, and something like a hatred of dogma, yet who also are inclined to musical ornament, and other paraphernalia of Divine service. From these facts, as well as from the growing ritual of the non-Episcopal Christians of this country, we may perceive that the unqualified breadth with which the argument has been drawn from ritual to doctrine in our discussions has evinced something of that precipitancy to which, from the narrow and insular character of his knowledge, as well as from the vigour of his will, the Englishman is particularly liable. Here also, from that deficiency which I have noted in the faculty of adapting the outward to the inward, he is apt to blunder into confounding what is appropriate and seemly with what partakes of excess or invidious meaning. At the same time, an important connection between high doctrine and high ritual is to be traced to a considerable extent in the Church of England, and in commenting on over-statement I do not seek to understate. This connection is, however, for the present hopelessly mixed with polemical considerations, and therefore excluded from the field of these remarks.

But there is a question, which it is the special purpose of this paper to suggest for consideration by my fellow-Christians generally, which is more practical and of greater importance, as it seems, to me, and has far stronger claims on the attention of the nation and of the rulers of the Church, than the question whether a handful of the clergy are or not engaged in an utterly hopeless and visionary effort to Romanise the Church and people of England. At no time since the sanguinary reign of Mary has such a scheme been possible. But if it had been possible in the seventeenth or eighteenth centuries, it would still have become impossible in the nineteenth; when Rome has subistituted for the proud boast of *semper eadem* a policy of violence and change in faith; when she has refurbished and paraded anew every rusty tool she was fondly thought to have disused; when no one can become her convert without renouncing his moral and mental freedom, and placing his civil loyalty and duty at the mercy of another; and when she has equally repudiated modern thought and ancient history. I cannot persuade myself to feel alarm as to the final issue of her crusades in England, and this although I do not undervalue her great powers of mischief. But there are questions of our own religious well-being that lie nearer home. And one of them is whether, as individuals, we can justly and truly say that the present movement in favour of ritual is a healthy movement for each of us; that is whether it gives or does not give us assistance in offering a more collected act of worship, when we enter the temple of the Most High, and think we go there to offer before Him the sacrifice of praise and prayer, and thanksgiving? Of one thing we may be quite certain, and it is this. To accumulate observances of ritual is to accumulate responsibility. It is the adoption of a higher standard of religious profession; and it requires a higher standard of religious practice. If we study, by appropriate or by rich embellishment, to make the Church more like the ideal of the House of God, and the services in it more impressive, by outward signs of His greatness and goodness, and of our littleness and meanness, all these are so many voices, audible and intelligible, though inarticulate, and to let them sound in our ears unheeded, is an offence against His majesty. If we are not the better for more ritual, we are the worse for it. A general augmentation of ritual, such as we see on every side around us, if it be without any corresponding enhancement of devotion, means more light, but not more love.

Indeed, it is even conceivable, nay far from improbable, that augmentation of ritual may import not increase but even diminution of fervour. Such must be the result in every case where the imagery of the eye and ear, actively multiplied, is allowed to draw off the energy, which ought to have its centre in the heart. There cannot be a doubt that the beauty of the edifice, the furniture, and the service, though their purpose be to carry the mind forward, may induce it to rest upon those objects themselves. Wherever the growth and progress of ritual, though that ritual be in itself suitable and proper, is accepted, whether consciously or unconsciously, and whether in whole or in part, by the individual, as standing in the stead of his own concentration and travail of spirit in devotion, there the ritual, though good in itself, becomes for him so much formality, that is so much deadness. Now there are multitudes of people who will accede at once to this proposition, who will even hold it to be no more than a truism, but with a complacent conviction, in the background of their minds, that it does not touch their case at all. They may be Presbyterians or Nonconformists; or they may be Churchmen whose clergyman preaches against Popery open or concealed, or who have themselves subscribed liberally to prosecute the Rev. this, or the Rev. that, for Ritualism. No matter. They, and their clergyman too, may nevertheless be flagrant Ritualists. For the barest minimum of ritual may be a screen hiding from the worshipper the Object of his worship: nay, will be such a screen, unless the worshipper bestirs himself to use it as a help, and to see that it is not a snare.

In the class of cases supposed, the ready aquiescence of a few moments back has by this time probably been converted into a wondering scepticism. And there is at first sight something of paradox in the assertion that all ritual, not only elaborate but modest, not only copious but scanty, has its dangers. It seems hard to preach suspicion and misgiving against what is generally approved or accepted by the most undeniable Protestants. But the very same person who errs by making his own conscience in ritual a measure for the consciences of other men, lest they should run to excess, may be himself in surfeit while he dooms them to starve, for what is famine to them may be to him excess: what they can assimilate may be to him indigestible. It is difficult, I think, to fix a maximum of ritual for all times and persons, and to predicate that all beyond the line must be harmful; but it is impossible to fix a minimum, and then to say, up to that point we are safe. No ritual is too much, provided it is subsidiary to the inner work of worship: and all ritual is too much, unless it ministers to that purpose.

If there be paradox in this assertion, the explanation of it is not far to seek. It will be found in the removal of a prevailing and dangerous error in kindred subject-matter. It is too commonly assumed that, provided only we repair to our church or our chapel, as the case may be, the performance of the work of adoration is a thing which may be taken for granted. And so it is, in the absence of unequivocal signs to the contrary, as between man and man. But not as between the individual man and his own conscience in the hour of self-review. If he knows anything of himself, and unless he be a person of singularly-favoured gifts, he will know that the work of Divine worship, so far from being a thing of course even among those who outwardly address themselves to its performance, is one of the most arduous which the human spirit can possibly set about. The processes of simple self-knowledge are difficult enough. All these, when a man worships, should be fresh in his consciousness: and this is the first indispensable condition for a right attitude of the soul before the footstool of the Eternal. The next is a frame of the affections adjusted on the one hand to this self-knowledge, and on the other to the attributes, and the more nearly felt presence, of the Being before Whom we stand. And the third is the sustained mental effort necessary to complete the act, wherein every Christian is a Priest; to carry our whole selves, as it were with our own hands, into that nearer Presence, and, uniting the humble and unworthy *prosphora* with the one full perfect and sufficient Sacrifice, to offer it upon the altar of the heart: putting aside every distraction of the outward sense, and endeavouring to complete the individual act as fully, as when in loneliness, after departing out of the flesh, we shall see eternal things no longer through but without a veil. Now, considering how we live, and must live, our common life in and by the senses, how all sustained mental abstraction is an effort, how the exercise of sympathy itself, which is such a power in Christian worship, is also a kind of bond to the visible; and, then, last of all, with what feebleness and fluctuation, not to say with what wayward duplicity, of intention we undertake the work, is it not too clear that in such a work we shall instinctively be too apt to remit our energies, and to slide unawares into mere perfunctory performance? And where and in proportion as the service of the body is more careful, and the exterior decency and solemnity of the public assembling more unimpeachable, these things themselves may contribute to form important elements of that inward self-complacency which makes it so easy for us, whenever we ourselves are judge and jury as well as 'prisoner at the bar,' to obtain a verdict of acquittal. In other words, the very things, which find their only sufficient warrant in their capacity and fitness to assist the work of inward worship, are particularly apt to be accepted by the individual himself as a substitute for inward worship, on account of that very capacity and fitness, of their inherent beauty and solemnity, of their peculiar and unworldly type. So that ritual, because it is full of uses, is also full of dangers. Though it is clear that men increase responsibility by augmenting it, they do not escape from danger by its diminution: nothing can make ritual safe except the strict observance of its purpose, namely, that it shall supply wings to the human soul in its callow efforts at upward flight. And, such being the meaning of true ritual, the just measure of it is to be found in the degree in which it furnishes that assistance to the individual Christian.

The changes, then, in our modes of performing Divine service ought to be answers to the inward call of minds advancing and working upwards in the great work of inward devotion. But when we see the extraordinary progress of ritual observance during the last generation, who is there that can be so sanguine as to suppose that there has been a corresponding growth of inward fervour, and of mental intelligence, in our general congregations? There is indeed a rule of simple decency to which, under all circumstances, we should strive to rise—for indecency in public worship is acted profanity, and is grossly irreligious in its effects. But when the standard of decency has once been attained, ought not the further steps to be vigilantly watched, I do not say by law, but by conscience? There are influences at work among us, far from spiritual, which may work in the direction of formalism through the medium of ritual. The vast amount of new made wealth in the country does not indeed lead to a display as profuse in the embellishment of the house of God, as in our own mansions, equipages, or dresses. Yet the wealthy, as such, have a preference for churches and for services with a certain amount of ornament: and it is quite possible that no small part of what we call the improvements in fabrics and in worship may be due simply to the demand of the richer man for a more costly article, and thus may represent not the spiritual growth but the materializing tendencies of the age. Again, there is a wider diffusion of taste among the many, though the faculty itself may not, with the few, have gained a finer edge; and, with this, the sense of the incongruous, and the grotesque, cannot but make some way. Here is another agency, adapted to improving the face and form of our religious services, without that which I would contend is the indispensable condition of all real and durable improvement—namely, a corresponding growth in the appreciation of the inward work of devotion. But a third and **very** important cause, working in the same direction, has been this. The standard of life and of devotion has risen among the clergy far more generally, and doubtless also more rapidly, than among the laity. It is more than possible that, in many instances, their own enlarged and elevated conception of what Divine service ought to be in order to answer the genuine demands of their own inward life, may have induced them to raise it in their several churches beyond any real capacity of their congregations to appreciate and turn it to account.

Even in the theatres of our day, the spectacle threatens to absorb the drama; and show, which should be the servant, to become the master. Much more is the danger real in the sanctuary, for the function of an audience is mainly passive, but that of a congregation is one of high and arduous, though unseen, activity.

But it is time to draw together the threads of this slight discourse upon a subject very far indeed from slight. Whatever may be said of the merits of authoritative and coercive repression in matters of ritual—and I am not very sanguine as to its effects—assuredly they never can dispense with the necessity, or perform the office, of the moral restraints of an awakened conscience. Some may be found to dispute the proposition that their gripe is hard, where a tender touch is needed; but who can question that they will reach but few, where many require a lesson? Attendance on religious services is governed among us to a great extent, especially in towns, and most of all in the metropolis, by fashion, taste, and liking: but no preference is really admissible in such a matter, except the strict answer of the conscious mind to the question, What degree and form of ritual is it that helps me, and what is it that hampers and impedes me, in the performance of the work for which all congregations of Christians assemble in their several churches?

If we consider the nature of Divine Service altogether at large, the presumption is against alteration, as such, in the manner of it. For the nature of God and the nature of man, and the relation of the one to the other, are constant; and in this solemn subject-matter, mere fashion, which is a principle of change questionable even in other departments, and which may be defined as change for its own sake, ought to have no place whatever. The varieties required by local circumstances or temperaments can be no novelties, and will probably in the lapse of time have asserted themselves sufficiently in the subsisting arrangements.

But if we limit and regulate our consideration of the case by a careful reference to our own time and country, the presumption is much weakened, possibly in one sense even reversed. For we have been emerging from a period in which the public worship of God had confessedly been reduced to a state of great external debasement. In this state of things a Reformation was necessary. Happily it came, and it surmounted the breakers and floods of prejudice. There was therefore a presumption not against, but in favour of change of some kind. When, however, the further question was reached of what kind the change ought to be, it remained true that each particular change required to be examined on its own merits, and to make its own case. The tests to be applied would, in language rather popular than correct, be such as the following questions might supply :—

1. Is it legally binding ? an inquiry, in which the element of desuetude cannot be absolutely excluded from the view of a clergyman or of his flock.

2. Is it in its own nature favourable to devout and intelligent adoration of God in the sanctuary ?

3. Will it increase, or will it limit, the active participation of the flock in the service ?

4. Is it conformable to the spirit of the Prayer-Book ?

5. Is it agreeable to the desires of this particular congregation ?

6. Is it adapted to their religious and their mental condition; and likely to bring them nearer to God in the act of worship, or to keep them further from Him; to collect or to disperse their thoughts, to warm or to freeze their affections?

It seems to me that, as a general rule, an answer to all these questions should be ready before a change in ritual is adopted: and that, where law interposes no impediment, still, if any of them has to be answered in the negative, such changes can hardly be allowable.

Except in the single case where the standard of decency has not been reached, I am wholly at a loss to conceive any excuse for contravening the general sense of a congregation by optional changes in ritual. If the clergyman thinks the matter to be one of principle, should he not instruct them? If he sees it to be one of taste and liking, should he not give way to them? Should he not be the first to perceive and hold that unsettlement in matters of religion is in itself no small evil: and to reflect that, by making precipitately some change which he approves, he may prepare the way and establish the precedent for a like precipitancy in other changes which he does not approve? Especially, what case can there be (except that of decency, and such a case can hardly be probable) in which he will be justified in repelling and dispersing his congregation for the sake of his service? Doubtless it is conceivable, that Divine Service may be rendered by careful ritual more suitable to the dignity of its purpose. But let us take, on the other hand, a church where a ritual thus improved has been forced upon a congregation to whom its provisions were like an unknown tongue, and whom it has therefore banished from the walls of the sanctuary. Is it conceivable that such a spectacle can be a pleasing one in the sight of the Most High? Did Christianity itself come down into the world in abstract perfection and in full development? or was it not rather opened on the world with nice regard to the contracted pupil of the human eye which it was gradually to enlarge, unfolding itself from day to day, in successive lessons of doctrine and event, here a little and there a little? The jewels in the crown of the Bride are the flocks within the walls of the temple; and men ever so hard of hearing are better than an empty bench.

I will, however, presume to express a favourable inclination towards one class of usages, with a corresponding aversion to their opposites. I heartily appreciate whatever, within the limits of the Prayer

Book, tends to augment the active participation of the laity in the services: as for example their joining audibly in the recital of the General Thanksgiving; or the aid they may give the clergyman (often so valuable even in a physical point of view) by reading the Lessons.*

Again, if ritual be on the increase among us, ought it not to receive at once its complement and (in one sense) its counterpoise, in a greater care, fervency, and power, of preaching? Nothing, in my opinion, is of more equivocal tendency than high ritual with a low appreciation of Christian doctrine. But if there be high ritual and sound doctrine too, these will not excuse inadequate appreciation or use of the power of the pulpit. If ritual does its work in raising the temper of devotion, it is a preparation for corresponding elevation in the work of the preacher: and if the preacher is able to warm, to interest, and to edify his hearers, then he improves their means of profiting by ritual, and arms them against its dangers.

* [I notice with pleasure that this practice has not yet suffered the blight of association with party. It is observed truly that there is no pointing of the clauses in the General Thanksgiving, as there is in the General Confession. But the epithet general, used in both cases, appears to suggest like practice in each; though I admit it may also mean a thanksgiving for blessings generally, as distinguished from particular blessings. Without presuming to give an opinion, I may be allowed to hope the practice is not illegal.]

But if self-will and want of consideration for others have been, and, in a diminished degree are still, a snare to the clergy, have not we of the laity the same infirmities with far less excuse? Is it not strange to see with what tenacity many a one of us will, when he casually attends a church other than his usual one, adhere to some usage or non-usage perfectly indifferent, but with the effect either of giving positive scandal or of exciting notice, that is, of distracting those around him from their proper work? How is this like the Apostle's rule, who was all things to all men? Or have we found out that the rules of Scripture were made, as well as the discipline of the Church, for the clergy alone? But even if it be the layman's privilege at once to rule the Church and to disobey it at his will, how is it that he does not respect the feelings of other laymen by decently conforming in all matters indifferent to the usages of the congregation to which he has chosen for the nonce to attach himself? It is much to be feared that when the clergyman has unlearned his own unreasonableness, he may still have to endure much from the unreasonableness of some handful of units among his flock. But if he be indeed worthy of his exalted office, he will see in the first place how little charity to the recalcitrant there will be in forcing on them even improvements which to them can only be stumblingblocks. Next, if he put on the armour of patience and of love, he will soon become aware of its winning efficacy. Lastly, there is an expedient which is in his own hands, and to which he cannot be prevented from resorting. Those defective perceptions of the outward manner of things, which I take to be national, must often make their mark on the clergy as well as on us of the laity. I remember long ago hearing a clergyman (who left the Church of England a few days later) complain of a want of reverence in his choir boys, with a demeanour, though it was in his beautiful church, fit for a tavern. The first, and last, and most effective article of ritual is deep reverence in the clergyman himself. Nothing can supply its place; and it will go far to supply the place of everything. It abhors affectation; and it does not consist in bowings and genuflexions, or in any definite acts: *nequeo monstrare, et sentio tantum.* The reason why this reverence is the most precious part of ritual, is because ritual in general consists *ex vi termini* in symbol; but reverence means, together with a sign, a thing signified. It lives and moves and has its being in a profound sense of the Divine presence, expressing itself through a suitable outward demeanour. But if the demeanour be without the sentiment, it is not reverence, it is only the husk and shell of reverence. The clergyman is necessarily the central point of his congregation. Their reverence cannot rise above his; and their everence will if insensibly yet continually approach his. If this be the key-note of the service, questions of ritual will adjust themselves in harmony with it. And one reason why the point may be more safely pressed is, because reverence need not be the property or characteristic of any school in particular. It distinguished the Margaret Chapel of forty years ago, when the pastors of that church were termed Evangelical. It subsisted in that same chapel thirty years ago, when Mr. Oakley (now alas! ours no more), and Mr. Upton Richards gave to its very simple services, such as would now scarcely satisfy an average congregation, and where the fabric was little less than hideous, that true solemnity which is in perfect concord with simplicity. The Papal Church now enjoys the advantages of the labours of Mr. Oakley; who united to a fine musical taste, a much finer and much rarer gift, in discerning and expressing the harmony between the inward purposes of Christian worship and its outward investiture, and who then had gathered round him a congregation the most devout and hearty that I (for one) have ever seen in any communion of the Christian world.

And now, for my last word, I will appeal to high authority.

In the fourteenth chapter of Saint Paul's First Epistle to the Corinthians may be found, what I would call the code of the New Testament upon ritual. The rules laid down by the Apostle to determine the comparative value of the gifts then so common in the Church will be found to contain the principles applicable to the regulation of Divine service; and it is touching to observe that they are immediately subjoined to that wonderful effusion describing "Charity," with which no ethical eloquence of Greece or Rome can suitably compare. The highest end, in the Apostle's mind, seems to be (v. 5) "that the church may receive edifying." At present there is a disposition to treat a handful of men as scapegoats; and my fear is not only that they may suffer injustice, but lest far wider evils, than any within their power to cause or cure, should creep onwards unobserved. As rank bigotry, and what is far worse, base egotistic selfishness may find their account, at moments like this, in swelling the cry of Protestantism, so much of no less rank worldliness may lurk in the fashionable tendency not only to excessive but even to moderate ritual. The best touchstone for dividing what is wrong and defining what is right in the exterior apparel of Divine service will be found in the holy desire and authoritative demand of the Apostle, "that the Church may receive edifying," rather than in abstract imagery of perfection on the one hand, or any form of narrow traditional prejudice on the other.

Note.—I subjoin to the article, now reprinted, Six Resolutions, in which, when the Public Worship Bill was before the House of Commons (July 1874), I endeavoured to set forth what appeared to me to offer a more safe and wise basis of legislation.

[1. That, in proceeding to consider the provisions of the bill for the Regulation of Public Worship, this House cannot do otherwise than take into view the lapse of more than two centuries since the enactment of the present Rubrics of the Common Prayer Book of the Church of England; the multitude of particulars embraced in the conduct of divine service under their provisions; the doubts occasionally attaching to their interpretation, and the number of points they are thought to leave undecided; the diversities of local custom which under these circumstances have long prevailed; and the unreasonableness of proscribing all varieties of opinion and usage among the many thousands of congregations of the Church distributed throughout the land.

2. That this House is therefore reluctant to place in the hands of every single Bishop, on the motion of one or of three persons howsoever

defined, greatly increased facilities towards procuring an absolute ruling of many points hitherto left open and reasonably allowing of diversity; and thereby towards the establishment of an inflexible rule of uniformity throughout the land, to the prejudice, in matters indifferent, of the liberty now practically existing.

3. That the House willingly acknowledges the great and exemplary devotion of the clergy in general to their sacred calling, but is not on that account the less disposed to guard against the indiscretion, or thirst for power, or other fault of individuals.

4. That the House is therefore willing to lend its best assistance to any measure recommended by adequate authority, with a view to provide more effectual securities against any neglect of or departure from strict law which may give evidence of a design to alter, without the consent of the nation, the spirit or substance of the established religion.

5. That, in the opinion of the House, it is also to be desired that the members of the Church, having a legitimate interest in her services, should receive ample protection against precipitate and arbitrary changes of established custom by the sole will of the clergyman, and against the wishes locally prevalent among them; and that such protection does not appear to be afforded by the provisions of the bill now before the House.

6. That the House attaches a high value to the concurrence of Her Majesty's Government with the ecclesiastical authorities in the initiative of legislation affecting the Established Church.]

IS THE CHURCH OF ENGLAND WORTH PRESERVING ? *

"*De vitâ et sanguine certant.*"
Æn. xii. 763.

A PAPER contributed to the CONTEMPORARY REVIEW for October, 1874, elicited, together with many expressions of interest and approval, many also of disappointment. There seemed to have been an expectation that the Essay might untie, or cut, the knot of the questions which had been so warmly, if not fiercely, agitated during the preceding Session of Parliament. But it had no such ambitious aim. Its object was, within the limited sphere of my means, simply to dispose men towards reflection, to substitute for the temper of the battle-field, good as in its place that may be, the temper of the chamber, where we commune with our own hearts, and are still. And this was done for two reasons; the first, because all true meditation is dispassionate, and a dispassionate mood is the first

* From *The Contemporary Review* for July, 1875.

indispensable condition for the resolution of controversies; the second, because there seemed to me to be real dangers connected, in the present day, with the merely fashionable accumulation of ritual, more subtle and very much more widely spread than the pronounced manifestations which had recently been so much debated.

The season is now tranquil; the furnace, no longer fed by the fuel of Parliamentary contentions among the highest authorities, has grown cool, and may be approached with safety, or, at least, with diminished risk. Those who opposed the Ecclesiastical Titles Bill, in 1851, in some cases had for their reward (as I have reason to know) paragraphs in "religious" newspapers, stating circumstantially that they had joined the Church of Rome. Those who questioned the Public Worship Act, in 1874, were more mildly, but as summarily, punished in being set down as Ritualists. In the heat of the period, it would have been mere folly to dispute the justice of the "ticketing," or classification. Perhaps it may now be allowed me to say, that I do not approach this question as a partisan. Were the question one between historical Christianity and systems opposed to or divergent from it, I could not honestly profess that I did not take a side. But as regards ritual, by which I understand the exterior forms of Divine Worship, I have never, at any time of my life, been employed in promoting its extension; never engaged in any either of its general or its local controversies. In the question of attendance at this church or that, I have never been governed by the abundance or the scantiness of its ritual, which I regard purely as an instrument, aiming at an end; as one of many instruments, and not as the first among them. To uphold the integrity of the Christian dogma, to trace its working, and to exhibit its adaptation to human thought and human welfare, in all the varying experience of the ages, is, in my view, perhaps the noblest of all tasks which it is given to the human mind to pursue. This is the guardianship of the great fountain of human hope, happiness, and virtue. But with respect to the clothing, which the Gospel may take to itself, my mind has a large margin of indulgence, if not of laxity, both ways. Much is to be allowed, I can hardly say how much, to national, sectional, and personal divergences, and to me it is indeed grievous to think that any range of liberty in these respects, which was respected during the storms of the sixteenth century should be denounced and threatened in the comparative calm of the nineteenth. Reverence, indeed, is a thing indispensable and invaluable; but reverence is one thing, and ritual another; and while reverence is preserved, I would never, according to my own inclination individually, quarrel with my brother about ritual. Nothing, therefore, would be easier than for me, after the manner of those who affect impartiality, to censure sharply the faults which, from our elevated point of view, we detect on both sides. Nothing easier, but few things more mischievous; for what is impartiality between the two, is often gross partiality and one-sidedness in the judgment of each, by reason of its ruthlessly shutting out of view those kernels of truth which are probably on both sides to be found under the respective husks of warring prejudice.

Without, however, any assumption of the tone of the critic or the pedagogue, there is one recommendation which may be addressed to both parties in the controversy of ritualism. They should surely be exhorted to cease altogether, or at least to reduce to its minimum, the practice of importing into questions concerning the externals of religion the element of doctrinal significance. The phrase is borrowed from a pamphlet by Dr. Trevor,* which bears the stamp, not only of ability, but of an independent mind. The topic is, in my belief, of deep moment. It cannot,

* "Trevor's Disputed Rubrics" (Parker), pp. 13 and *seqq.*

perhaps, be more effectively illustrated than by a reference to the particular article of ritual which has been, more than any other, the subject of recent contest—namely, the question whether, during the prayer of consecration in the Office of Communion, the priest shall stand with his face towards the East, or towards the South.

By some mental process, which it seems difficult for an unbiassed understanding to comprehend, a controversy, which may almost be called furious, has been raised on this matter. It of course transcends —indeed, it almost scorns—the bounds of the narrower question, whether the one or the other posture is agreeable, or, as may perhaps better be said, is more agreeable, to the legal prescriptions of the rubrics. For it is held, and held on both sides by persons not inconsiderable either in weight or number, that, if the priest looks eastwards at this point of the service, he thereby affirms the doctrines of the Real Presence and the Eucharistic Sacrifice, but that, if on the contrary he takes his place at the north end of the altar or table, he thereby puts a negative on those doctrines. If the truth of this contention be admitted, without doubt the most formidable consequences may then be apprehended from any possible issue of the debate. It is idle to hope that even judges can preserve the balance of their minds when the air comes to be so thickly charged with storm. We may say almost with certainty that there are many now reckoned as members of the Church of England, whom, on the one side, the affirmation of those principles would distract and might displace, while, on the other, their negation would precipitate a schism of an enduring character. But if this be even partially true, does it not elevate into an imperious duty, for all right-minded men, that which is in itself a rule of reason—namely, that we should steadily resolve not to annex to any particular acts of external usage a special dogmatic interpretation, so long as they will naturally and unconstrainedly bear some sense not entailing that consequence?

Now, it seems pretty evident that, in the present instance, the contentions of each of the two parties are perfectly capable of being explained and supported upon grounds having no reference to the doctrines, with which they have been somewhat wilfully placed in a connection as stringent, and perhaps as perilous, as that of the folds of the boa-constrictor. Take, for example, the case in favour of what we may be allowed to call orientation. The bishops of the Savoy Conference laid down the principle, as one

* "Trevor's Disputed Rubrics" (Parker), pp. 13 and *seqq.*

founded in general propriety and reason, that when the minister addresses the people he should turn himself towards them, as, for example, in preaching or in reading the lessons from Holy Scripture; but that when, for and with them, he addresses himself to God, there is solecism and incongruity in his being placed as if he were addressing them. The natural course, then, they held to be, that congregation and minister, engaged in a common act, should, unless conformity between the inward and the outward is to be entirely expelled from the regulation of human demeanour, look together in a common direction. When this is done by a clergyman reading the Litany at a faldstool, he commonly turns his back on part of the congregation, and part of the congregation on him. When the same rule is followed in the prayer of consecration, the back of the clergyman is turned towards the entire congregation only from the circumstance that he officiates at the extreme East end of the church. The proper idea of the position is, not that he turns his back on the congregation, but that, placed at the head of the congregation, and acting for as well as with them in the capacity of the public organ of the assembled flock, he and they all turn in the same direction, and his back is towards the whole only as the back of the first line of worshippers behind him is towards all their fellow-worshippers. He simply does that, which every one does in sitting or standing at the head of a column or body of men. And if he be a believer in the Real Presence and the Eucharistic Sacrifice, woe be to him in that capacity, unless he has some other and firmer defence for these doctrines than the assumed symbolism of an attitude that he shares with so many Protestant clergyman of Continental Europe, who are known to be bound but little to the first, and are generally adverse to the second of these doctrines. Thus, then, we have, in a particular view of the mere proprieties of the case, a perfectly adequate explanation of the desire to assume the eastward position, without any reference whatever to any given doctrinal significance, be it cherished or be it obnoxious. Let us now turn to the other side of the question, and see whether similar reasoning will not hold good.

It does not follow, upon the expulsion of this transcendental element from the discussion, that the objector to the plan of facing eastwards is left without a case, which again is one of simple policy and expediency, from his own point of view. He may, like many of his countrymen, be so wanting in the rudiments of the æsthetic sense, as to think that the most advantageous position for a Christian pastor towards the people is that in which he speaks all the prayers straight into their faces, and the best arrangement for the flock that of the double pews, in which they are set to look at one another through the service, in order to correct, by mutual contemplation, any excessive tendency to rapt and collected devotion. But it is not necessary to impute to him this irrational frame of mind. He may admit that in the act of prayer, as a rule, minister and people may advantageously look in the same direction. He may renounce the imputation upon his adversaries that, by facing eastwards, they express adhesion to certain doctrines. And he may still point out that there is more to be said. The prayer of consecration is a prayer not of petition only, but of action too. In the course of it, by no less than five parenthetical rubrics, the priest is directed to perform as many manual acts; and, quite apart from the legal argument that the reference in the principal rubric to breaking the bread before the people requires the action to be performed in their view, he may contend, if he thinks fit, that for the better comprehension of the service, it is well that they should have the power of seeing all that is required of the priest respecting the handling of the sacred elements, and that this cannot be seen, or cannot so well be seen, if he faces eastwards, as if, standing at the north end of the holy table, he faces towards the south. I do not enter into the question whether this argument be conclusive, either as to the legal interpretation of the rubric, with which at present we have nothing to do, or as to the advantage of actual view and the comparative facilities for allowing it. It is enough to show that arguments may be made in perfect good faith, and free from anything irrational, against as well as for the eastward position, without embracing the embittering element of doctrinal significance; that both from the one side and the other the question may be reasonably debated on general grounds of religious expediency. For if this be so, it becomes in a high degree impolitic, and very injurious to the interests of religion, to fasten upon these questions of position, whether in the sense of approval or of repudiation, significations which they do not require, and which they will only so far bear that, by prejudice or association, we can in any given case assign to words and things a colour they do not of themselves possess. There are surely enough real occasions for contention in the world to satisfy the most greedy appetite, without adding to them those which are conventional; that is to say, those where the contention is not upon the things themselves, but upon the constructions which prejudice or passion may attach to them. Surely if a Zuinglian could persuade himself that the English Communion Office was founded upon the basis of Zuinglian ideas, he would act weakly and inconsistently should he renounce the ministry of the Church because he was ordered to face eastwards during the prayer of consecration; and at least as surely would one, believing in the Catholic and primitive character of the office, be open to similar blame if he in like manner repudiated his function as a priest upon being required to take his place only on the North. Preferences for the one or the other position it is easy to conceive. To varying ideas of worship—and in these later times the idea of worship does materially vary—the one or the other may seem, or may even be, more thoroughly conformable; but strange indeed, in my view, must be the composition of the mind which can deliberately judge that the position at the North end is in itself irreverent, or that facing towards the East is in itself superstitious. Both cannot be right in a dispute, but both may be wrong; and one of the many ways in which this comes about is when the thing contended for is, by a common consent in error, needlessly lifted out of the region of things indifferent into that of things essential, and a distinction, founded originally on the phantasy of man, becomes the *articulus stantis aut cadentis concordiæ.*

It sometimes seems as though, even in the tumult of the Reformation, when the fountains of the great deep were broken up, the general mind must yet have been more solid and steadier, perhaps even more charitable, than now; though the edge of controversies at that epoch was physical as well as moral, and involved, at every sweep of the weapon, national defence and the personal safety or peril of life and limb. Members of the Church of England, even now somewhat irreverent as a body with reference to kneeling in ordinary worship, are nevertheless all content to kneel in the act of receiving the Holy Communion; a most becoming, most soothing, most fraternal usage. General censure would descend upon the man who should attempt to disturb it by alleging that this humble attitude of obeisance too much favoured the idea of paying worship to the consecrated elements. No less certainly, and even more sharply, would he be condemned who, himself believing in the Real Presence, should endeavour to force it home on others as the only key to the meaning of the usage. But who can fail to see that for minds, I will not say jaundiced, but preoccupied with the disposition to attach extreme constructions to outward acts in the direction in which they seem to lean, nothing is more easy than to annex to the kneeling attitude of the receiver in the Holy

Eucharist the colour and idea of adoration of the consecrated elements? So, also, nothing would be more difficult than, when once such a colour has been so annexed, again to detach it effectually, and thus to bring the practice to an equitable judgment. Yet the Church of England, which has unitedly settled down upon the question of kneeling at reception, has resolutely thrust aside the extreme construction, through which a baleful concurrence of opposing partisans might have rendered it intolerable. And this she did, carrying the practice itself without shock or hesitation through all the fluctuations of her Liturgy, during times when theological controversy was exasperated by every mundane passion which either the use of force, or its anticipation, can arouse. It will indeed be strange—should we not rather say it will indeed be shameful—if, after conducting the desperate struggles of the Reformation to their issue, and when we have realized its moral and social fruits for three centuries and a half, we prove to be so much less wise and less forbearing than our less civilized and refined forefathers, that we are to be led, by an aggravated misuse of this practice of gratuitous construction, to create a breach upon a question so much less difficult, so much less calling for or warranting extreme issues, than that which they proved themselves able to accommodate?

It may indeed be said, and not untruly, that in a certain sense both the friends and the adversaries of the practice I have been considering are agreed in attaching to it the meaning I presume to deprecate. Where both parties to a suit are agreed, it is idle, we may be told, to dispute what they concur in. Now the very point I desire to bring into clear view is that this is not a suit with two parties to it, but that many, perhaps most, of those who are entitled to be heard, are not before the court; many, aye multitudes, who think either this question should be let alone, or that if it is not let alone, it should be decided upon dry and cold considerations of law, history, and science, so far as they are found to inhere in it; not judged by patches of glaring colour, the symbols of party, which are fastened upon it from without. If this be a just view, the concurrence of the two parties named above in their construction of the eastward position is no better a reason for the acquiescence of the dispassionate community, than the agreement of two boys at school or in the street to fight, in order to ascertain who is the strongest, is a reason against the interference of bystanders to stop them if they can.

There is in political life a practice analogous, as it seems to me, to the practice of needlessly importing doctrinal significance into discussions upon ceremonial.

It is indeed a very common fashion to urge that something, in itself good and allowable, has become bad and inadmissible on account of motives imputed to those who ask it. The Reforms proposed in 1831 and 1866 were not to be conceded, because they would be used as levers for ulterior extensions of the franchise. The Irish Church was not to be disestablished, because the change would serve as an argument for disestablishing the Church of England. Irish public-houses must not be closed on Sunday where the people desire it, for fear the measure should bring about a similar closing in England, where public opinion is not ripe for it. But then, in the secular world, this very practice is taken as the indication of an illiberal mind, and a short-sighted policy. The truly liberal maxim has ever been that by granting just claims you disarm undue demands: that things should be judged as they are in themselves, and not in the extraneous considerations, and remote eventualities, which sanguine friends and bitter foes oftentimes agree in annexing to them. It is, therefore, with unfeigned surprise, that I read in the work of no mean writer on this rubrical controversy, that in May last he "prayed" that the priest might be allowed to face eastwards, but that he would now refuse it, because "this eastward position is claimed for distinctively doctrinal purposes." I am reluctant to cite a respected name, but it is necessary to give the means of verifying my statement by a reference to Dr. Swainson's "Rubrical Question of 1874,"* pp. 1, 5. I might, I believe, add other instances of the same unfortunate line of thought; but it is needless, and I gladly refrain.

What, then, is the upshot of this extraordinary preference of the worse over the better, the more arbitrary over the direct and inherent construction? It is this, that it heats the blood and quickens the zeal of sympathizing partisans. But then it has exactly the same effect upon the partisans of the two opposite opinions. So that it widens breaches, feeds the spirit of mutual defiance, and affords, like abundant alcohol, an intoxicating satisfaction, to be followed by the remorse of the morrow when the mischief has been done. It enhances the difficulties of the Judge's task, and makes hearty acquiescence in his decisions almost hopeless.

Wherever this importation of doctrinal significance, I care not from which side, has been effected, it powerfully tends to persuade the worsted party that the law has been strained against him on grounds

---

* But, at p. 70, Dr. Swainson, with great candour, states that, if the law be declared adversely to his view, he will at once renounce this imputation of doctrinal significance.

extraneous to the argument, and to drive him either upon direct disobedience, or upon circuitous modes of counteracting the operation of any Judgment given. Those against whom the letter of the law seems to be turned invidiously, are apt to think they may freely and justly avail themselves of it wherever it is in their favour. Supposing, for example, that, by a judgment appearing to rest on considerations of policy and not of law, the eastward position were to be condemned, who does not see that those who thought themselves wronged might discover ample means of compensation ? Some have contended that the clergy, sustained by their flocks, might retrench the services of the parish church; and that, offering within its walls a minimum both of ritual and of the opportunities of worship, they might elsewhere institute and attend services which, under a recent Statute (18 & 19 Vict. c. 86), they believe they might carry on without being subject to the restraints of the Act of Uniformity. I am not aware that this contention can be confuted. If not, it opens to view a real and serious danger.

Or again, in the churches themselves, where the clergyman was forbidden to adopt a position construed as implying an excessive reverence, not he only, but, with certain immunity from consequences, his congregation might, and probably would, resort to other external acts, at least as effectual for the same purpose, much more closely related to doctrinal significance, much more conspicuous in themselves, and, perhaps, much more offensive to fellow-worshippers, than the position which had been prohibited. What, upon either of these suppositions, would have been gained by the most signal victory in the courts, either for truth or for peace, or even for the feelings and objects of those who would be called the winners?

I have dwelt at length on this particular subject, not because I imagine the foregoing remarks to offer a solution of existing difficulties, but in order to point out and to avert, if possible, what would make a solution impossible. The very first condition of healthy thought and action is an effort at self-mastery, and the expulsion, from the controversies concerning certain rubrics, of considerations which aggravate those controversies into hopelessness, and which seem to dwell in them, as demons dwelt in the bodies of the possessed, till they were expelled by the beneficent Saviour, and left the sufferers at length restored to their right mind. If we cannot fulfil this first condition of sanity, it is, I fear, hopeless to expect that the day of doom for the Established Church of England can be long postponed. It is bad enough, in my opinion, that we should have to adjust these difficulties by the necessarily rude and coarse machinery of Courts of law. I do not disguise my belief, founded on very long and rather anxious observation, that the series of penal proceedings in the English Church during the last forty years, which, virtually though not technically, began with the action of the University of Oxford against Bishop Hampden, have as a whole been mischievous. I make no accusation, in speaking thus, against those who have promoted them. I will not say that they have been without provocation, that they could easily have been avoided, that they have been dishonourably instituted, or even vindictively pursued. I do not inquire whether, when they have been strictly judicial, they have or have not generally added to the fame of our British Judicature for power or for learning. Unhappily they came upon a country little conversant with theological, historical, or ecclesiastical science, and a country which had not been used for three hundred years, with the rarest exceptions, to raise these questions before the tribunals. The only one of them, in which I have taken a part, was the summary proceeding of the Council of King's College against Mr. Maurice. I made an ineffectual endeavour, with the support of Judge Patteson and Sir B. Brodie, and the approval of Bishop Blomfield, to check what seemed to me the unwise and ruthless vehemence of the majority which dismissed that gentleman from his office. It may be that, in this or that particular case, a balance of good over evil may have resulted. It could not but be that in particular instances some who would not have wished them to be instituted, could not wish them to fail. But I have very long been convinced that, as a whole, they have exasperated strife and not composed it; have tempted men to employ a substitute, at once violent and inefficient, for moral and mental force; have aggravated perils which they were honestly intended to avert; have impaired confidence, and shaken the fabric of the Church to its foundations.

The experience of half a century ago may, in part, serve to illustrate an opinion which may have startled many of my readers, but which long ago I for one entertained and made known in quarters of great influence. Nothing could be sharper than was at that time the animosity of Churchmen in general against what are termed Evangelical opinions. There was language used about them and their proposers in works of authority—such, for instance, as certain tracts of the Society for Promoting Christian Knowledge—which was not only insolent, but almost libellous. But it seems that the Church took to heart the wise counsel which Athene offered to Achilles, that he should abuse Agamemnon, but not touch him. "Fall foul of him with words, as much as you have a mind: but keep your sword within the scabbard." * The sword, at that period of our Church history, was never drawn; and the controversy settled itself in an advantageous way. Are we driven to admit that there was, among the rulers and the ruled of those days, more of patience, or of faith in moral force, or both; more of the temper of Gamaliel, and less of the temper of Saul?

At a later date, it is true that Bishop Philpotts broke the tradition of this pacific policy in the case of Mr. Gorham. But all who knew that remarkable Prelate are aware that he was a man of sole action, rather than of counsel and concert; and it was an individual, not a body, that was responsible for striking the blow, of which the recoil so seriously strained the Church of England.

While frankly avowing the estimate I form of the results which have flowed from these penal proceedings in matter belonging to law undoubtedly, but to conscience as well as law, I am far from believing that the public as yet fully shares these views. I must suppose, especially after the legislative proceedings of last year, that my countrymen are well satisfied with the general

---

* II. i. 210.

or average results, and have detected in them what my eyesight has not perceived—a tendency to compose the troubles, and consolidate the fabric, of the Church. My ambition does not, then, soar so high as to ask for a renunciation of the comforts and advantages of religious litigation. All that I am now contending for is that the suits which may be raised ought not to be embittered by the opening of sources of exasperation that do not properly belong to them; that contribute absolutely nothing to the legal argument on either side for the elucidation of the rubrics; and that, on the contrary, by inflaming passion, and suggesting prejudice, darken and weaken the intellects, while they excite the sensibilities, of all concerned.

If, as I hope, I may have carried with me some degree of concurrence in the main proposition I have thus far urged, let us now turn to survey a wider prospect. Let us look for a while at the condition of the English Church—its fears and dangers on the one hand, its powers and capacities on the other; and let us then ask ourselves whether duty binds and prudence recommends us to tear it in pieces, or to hold it together.

It is necessary first to free the inquiry from a source of verbal misunderstanding. In one and the same body, we see two aspects, two characters, perfectly distinct. That body declares herself, and is supposed by the law of the country to be, the ancient and Catholic Church of the country, while it is also the national Establishment of Religion. In the first capacity, it derives its lineage and commission from our Saviour and the Apostles; in the second, it is officered and controlled by the State. We may speak of holding the Church together, or of holding the Church and the State together. I am far from placing the two duties on the same ground, or assigning to them a common elevation. Yet the subjects are, in a certain form, closely connected; and the form is this. It may be that the continuing union of the Church within herself will not secure without limit the continuing union of the Church with the State. But it is certain, nevertheless, that the splitting of the Church will destroy its union with the State. Not only as a Church, but as an endowed Establishment, it is, without doubt, still very strong. Sir Robert Peel said, over a quarter of a century ago, in discussing the emancipation of the Jews, that the only dangers of the Church consisted in its internal divisions. Within that quarter of a century the dangers have increased, but with them has probably increased also the strength to bear them. Menace and peril from without, against the Church as an Establishment, have made ground, but are still within measure. They still represent a minor, not a major, social force; though they are seconded by a general movement of the time, very visible in other countries, and apparently pervading Christendom at large, yet with a current certainly slow, perhaps indefinitely slow. But though the Church may be possessed of a sufficient fund of strength, there is no redundancy that can be safely parted with. Any secession, if of sensible amount, constituting itself into a separate body, would operate on the National Church, with reference to its nationality, like a rent in a wall, which is mainly important, not by the weight of material it detaches, but by the discontinuity it leaves.

It is not, indeed, only the severance of the Church into two bodies which might precipitate disestablishment. Obstinacy and exasperation of internal strife might operate yet more effectively towards the same end. The renewal of scenes and occurrences like those of the session of 1874 would be felt, even more heavily than on that first occasion, to involve not only pain, but degradation. The disposition of some to deny to the members of the National Church the commonest privileges belonging to a religious communion, the determination of others to cancel her birthright for a mess of pottage, the natural shrinking of the better and more refined minds from indecent conflict, the occasional exhibition of cynicism, presumption, ignorance, and contumely, were, indeed, relieved by much genial good sense and good feeling, found, perhaps, not least conspicuously among those, who were by religious profession most widely severed from the National Church. But the mischief of one can inflict wounds on a religious body, which the abstinence and silent disapproval of a hundred cannot heal; and, unless an English spirit has departed wholly from the precincts of the English Church, she will, when the outrage to feeling grows unendurable, at least in the persons of the most high-minded among her children, absolutely decline the degrading relation to which not a few seem to think her born. I pass, then, to consider whether it be a duty or not to keep the Church united, with the negative assumption implied in these remarks, that without such union there cannot be a reasonable hope of saving the Establishment.

But it may be said, what is this internal union of the Church, which is professed to be of such value? We have within it men who build, or suppose themselves to build, their religion only upon their private judgment, unequally yoked with those who acknowledge the guiding value of Christian history and witness; men who believe in a visible Church, and men who do not; men who desire a further Reformation, and men who think the Reformation we have had already went too far; men who think a Church exists for the custody and teaching of the truth, and men who view it as a magazine for the collection and parade of all sorts of opinions, to meet the tastes of all sorts of customers. Nay, besides all this, are there not those who, with such concealment only as prudence may require, question the authority of Holy Scripture, and doubt, or dissolve into misty figure, even the cardinal facts of our redemption enshrined in the Apostles' Creed? What union, compatible with the avowed or unavowed existence of these diversities, can deserve the name, or can be worth paying a price to maintain?

Now, before we examine the value or no value of this union, the first question is—does it exist, and how and where does it exist, as a fact? It does; and it is to be found in the common law, common action and history, common worship, and probably, above all, the common Manual of worship, in the Church. Though it is accompanied with many divergencies of dogmatic leaning, and though these differences are often prosecuted with a lamentable bitterness, yet in the law, the history, the worship, and the Manual, they have a common centre, to which, upon the whole, all, or nearly all, the members of the body are really and strongly, though it may be not uniformly nor altogether consistently, attached, and which is at once distinctive, and in its measure efficient. Nay, more, it has been stated in public, and I incline to believe with truth, that the rubrics of the Church are at this moment more accurately followed than at any period of her history since the Reformation. Twelve months ago I scandalized the tender consciences of some by pointing out that in a law which combined the three conspicuous features of being extremely minute, very ancient, and in its essence not prohibitive but directory, absolute and uniform obedience was hardly to be expected, perhaps, in the strict meaning of the terms, hardly even to be desired. I admit the scandals of division, and the greater scandals of dissension; but there are, as I believe, fifteen millions of people in this country who have not thrown off their allegiance to its Church, and these people, when they speak of it, to a great extent mean the same thing, and, when they resort to it, willingly concur in the same acts; willingly, on the whole, though the different portions of them each abate something from their individual preferences to meet on common ground, as Tories, Whigs, and Radicals do the like, to meet on the common ground of our living and working constitution. This union, then, I hold to be a fact, and I contend that it is a fact worth preserving. I do not beg that question: I only aver that it is the question really at issue; and I ask that it may be dispassionately considered, for many questions of conduct depend upon it.

The duty of promoting union in religion is elevated by special causes at the present day into a peculiar solemnity; while these causes also envelop it in an extraordinary intricacy. The religion of Christ as a whole, nay, even the pallid scheme of Theism, is assailed with a sweep and vehemence of hostility greater probably than at any former period. While the war thus rages without the wall, none can say that the reciprocal antagonism of Christian bodies is perceptibly mitigated within it, or that the demarcating spaces between them are narrower than they were. Most singular of all, the greatest of the Christian communions, to say nothing of the smaller, are agitated singly and severally by the presence or proximity of internal schism. The Papal Church has gone to war with portions of its adherents in Armenia, in Germany, in Italy, in Switzerland, and elsewhere; besides being in conflict with the greater number of Christian States, especially of those where the Roman religion is professed. The relations of the Church of England beyond St. George's Channel, however euphemistically treated in some quarters, are dark, and darkening still. Even the immovable East is shaken. The Sclavonic, and the Hellenic, or non-Sclavonic, elements are at present, though without doctrinal variance, yet in sharp ecclesiastical contention ; and a formidable schism in Bulgaria, not discountenanced by Russian influences, disturbs at its own doors the ancient and venerable See of Constantinople, with its sister Patriarchates. This is a rude and slight, but I believe an accurate outline. I do not say it carries us beyond, but it certainly carries up to this point : that now, more than ever, our steps should be wary and our heads cool, and that, if we should not disguise the full significance of controversies, neither should we aggravate them by pouring Cayenne pepper into every open wound.

I do not say that, in circumstances like these, it becomes the duty of each man to sacrifice everything for the internal unity of his own communion. When that communion, by wanton innovation, betrays its duty, and agravates the controversies of Christendom, the very best friend to its eventual unity may be he who at all hazards, and to all lengths, resists the revolutionary change. But it would seem that in all cases where the religious body to which we belong has not set up the *petra scandali*, the presumptive duty of the individual who remains in its communion, to study its peace, is enhanced. Nowhere, in my view, does this proposition apply with such force as to the case of the English Church. This Church and nation, by an use of their reforming powers, upon the whole wonderfully temperate, found for themselves, amidst the tempests of the sixteenth and seventeenth centuries, a haven of comparative tranquillity, from which, for more than two centuries, they have not been dislodged. Within this haven it has, especially of late years, been amply proved that every good work of the Divine Kingdom may be prosecuted with effect, and every quality that enlarges and ennobles human character may be abundantly reared. I do not now speak of our British Nonconformists, for whom I entertain a very cordial respect: I confine myself to what is still the National Church; and I earnestly urge it upon all her members that the more they study her place and function in Christendom, the more they will find that her unity, qualified but real, is worth preserving.

I will dwell but very lightly on the arguments which sustain this conclusion. They refer first to the national office of this great institution. It can hardly be described better than in a few words which I extract from a recent article in the *Edinburgh Review* :—

"The crown and flower of such a movement was the Elizabethan Church of England. There the watchword was never destruction or innovation; there a simple, Scriptural, Catholic, and objective teaching has preserved us from superstitious and dogmatic vagaries on the one hand, and from the subjective weakness of many of the Protestant sects on the other. To the formation of such a Church the nation gave its strength and its intelligence, viz., that of the idea of More (?), of Shakespeare, and of Bacon; and what is more, the whole nation contributed its good sense, its sobriety, its steadfastness, and its appreciation of a manly and regulated freedom."—*Edinburgh Review*, April, 1875, p. 574.

There are those who think that bold changes in the law and constitution of the Church, in the direction of developed Protestantism, would bring within its borders a larger proportion of the people. My own opinion is the reverse of this. I look upon any changes whatever, especially of the Prayer-Book, if sensible in amount and contentious in character, as simply synonymous with the destruction of the National Establishment. But the matter is one of opinion only; and I fully admit the title of the nation to make any such changes, if they think fit, with such a purpose in view.

But, besides her national office and capabilities, the Church of England, in her higher character as a form of the Christian religion, has a position at once most perilous and most precious (I here borrow the well-known expression of De Maistre) with reference to Christendom at large. She alone, of all Churches, has points of contact, of access, of sympathy, touching upon all the important sections of the Christian commonwealth. Liable, more than any other religious body, to see her less stable or more fastidious members drop off from her now in this direction and now in that, she is, nevertheless, in a partial but not an unreal sense, a link of union between the several fractions of the Christian body. At every point of her frontier, she is in close competition with the great Latin communion, and with the varied, active, and in no way other than respectable, forms of Nonconformity. Nor does this represent the whole of the danger which, as to her sectional interests, she daily suffers in detail. She inhabits a sphere of greater social activity than is found in any other country of Europe; she is in closer neighbourhood, throughout her structure, than any other Church, with the spirit of inquiry (I do not say of research), and is proportionably more liable to defections in the direction of unbelief, or, if that word be invidious, of non-belief or negation. But this great amount of actual peril and besetting weakness is, in at least a corresponding degree, potential force and usefulness, for others as well as for herself; and no philosophic observer, whatever be his leanings, can exclude her from a prominent place in his survey of Christendom.

These things, it seems to me, are not enough considered among us. If they were enough considered, we should be less passionate in our internal controversies. We should recollect that we hold what all admit to be, a middle place; that the strain, as in a wheel, is greatest at the centre, the tendency to dislocation there most difficult to subdue. So we should more contentedly accept the burdens of the position, for the sake of the high, disinterested, and beneficent mission with which they seem to be allied. Even if I am wrong in the persuasion that much ought to be borne rather than bring about a rupture, I can hardly be wrong in claiming the assent of all to the proposition that we had better not prosecute our controversies wildly and at haphazard, but that we should carefully examine, before each step is taken, what other steps it will bring after it, and what consequences the series may as a whole involve.

I am quite aware of the answer which will spring to the lips of some. "The object of the long series of prosecutions, and of the Act of 1874, is to cut out a gangrene from the Church of England; to defeat a conspiracy which aims at reversing the movement of the Reformation, and at remodelling her tenets, her worship, and her discipline, on the basis of the Papal Church: aye, even with all the aggravations of her earlier system, which that Church has in the latter times adopted." But the answer to this answer is again perfectly ready. If there be within the Church of England a section of clergy or of laity, which is engaged in such a conspiracy, it is one extremely, almost infinitesimally small. I do not now deal with the very different charge against doctrines and practices which are said to *tend* towards the Church of Rome. This charge was made against Laud by the Puritans, and is made against the Prayer-Book at large by our Nonconforming friends, or by very many of them.* My

---

* These allegations did not commence with the revivals of our time. See for example the following extract from "The Catholic Question: addressed to the Freeholders of the County of York;" on the General Election of 1826: p. 24.

"All these things, however, are visible in the Church of England: go to a cathedral, hear and see all the magnificent things done there: behold the regiments of wax tapers, the white-robed priests, the macebearers; the chaunters, the picture over the altar, the wax-lights and the burnished gold plates and cups on the altar; then listen to the prayers repeated in chaunt, the anthems, the musical responses, the thundering of the organ and the echoes of the interminable roof; and then say, is not this idolatry? it is all the idolatry that the Catholics admit; it is the natural inclination that we have to those weak and beggarly elements,

point is that those, who *aim* at Romanizing the Church, are at worst a handful. If, then, the purpose be to put them down, isolate them; attack them (since you think it worth while) in the points they distinctively profess and practise. But is this the course actually taken? Are these points the subjects of the recent prosecutions, of the present threats, of the crowd of pamphlets and volumes upon ritual controversy, which daily issue from the press? On the contrary, these prosecutions, these menaces, these voluminous productions, have always for their main, and often for their exclusive, subject the two points of Church law which relate to the position of the consecrator, and to the rubric on ecclesiastical vestments. But now we arrive at a formidable dilemma. Upon the construction of the law on these two points, the prosecuting parties are at variance, not with a handful, but with a very large number, with thousands and tens of thousands, both of the

pomp and pride; and which both Catholics and the High Church party think so important in religion. I boldly assert that there is more idolatry in the Church of England than amongst the English Catholics; and for this simple reason, because the Church of England can better afford it. Two-thirds of the Church service is pomp and grandeur; it is as Charles II. used to say, 'the service of gentlemen.' It is for show, and for a striking impression; the cathedral service *is nothing more or less than a mass*, for it is all chaunted from beginning to end, and the people cannot understand a word of it."

clergy and the laity of the Church of England, whose averments I understand to be these: first, that the law of 1662, fairly interpreted, enjoins the vestments of the First Prayer Book of Edward VI., and the eastward position of the consecrating priest; secondly, that it would be inequitable and unwise to enforce these laws, and that the prevailing liberty should continue; thirdly, that it would be inequitable and unwise to alter them. Are these propositions conclusive evidence of a conspiracy to assimilate the Reformed religion of England to the Papal Church? If they are not, why is the war to be conducted mainly, and thus hotly, in the region they define? If they are, then our position is one of great danger, because it is well known that a very large and very weighty portion of the clergy, with no inconsiderable number of the laity, proceeding upon various grounds—love of ritual, love of liberty, dread of rupture—are arrayed on the side of toleration against the prosecuting party. It is said to have been declared by persons in high authority, that a large portion of both clergy and laity do entertain the desire to Romanize the Church. I am convinced it is not so; but if it be so, our condition is indeed formidable, and we are preparing to "shoot Niagara." For I hold it to be beyond dispute that, whether minor operations of the knife be or be not safe for us, large excisions, large amputations, are what the constitution of the patient will not bear. Under them the Establishment will part into shreds; and even the Church may undergo sharp and searching consequences, which as yet it would be hardly possible to forecast, either in principle or detail.

For the avoidance of these dangers, my long cherished conviction still subsists that the best and most effectual remedy is to be found in more largely forbearing to raise contentious issues, and in ceasing to aim at ruling consciences by courts. I say this is the most effectual remedy. For the next best, which is that the parties shall, after full and decisive exposition of the law, submit to the sentence of the tribunals, is manifestly at the least incomplete. The prosecuting party, in the two matters of the Rubric on Vestments and the position of the consecrating minister, will doubtless submit to an adverse judgment; but will as certainly, and not without reason from its own point of view, transfer to the legislative arena the agitations of the judicial forum. The Dean of Bristol, who has argued these questions with his usual force and directness, wishes that no alterations should be made in the rubrics, if what is called the Purchas judgment be maintained; but, with his acute eye, he has perhaps shrewd suspicions on that subject; and accordingly he says, if that judgment be not maintained, he is "for such wide agitation, such strong and determined measures, as shall compel [sic] the Legislature to give back to the Church its old and happy character of purity."* A pleasant prospect for our old age! But the Dean has this advantage over me. He does not object to the *voies de fait*, and, if only the judgment goes his way, will be quite happy. I am one of those who have the misfortune of being like Falkland in the war of King and Parliament: I shall deplore all disturbing Judgments on the points in question, wholly irrespective of my own sympathies or antipathies. If the prosecutors are defeated, who are strongly (to use a barbarous word) establishmentarian, we shall have agitation for a change in the law, too likely to end in rupture. If they succeed (which I own I find it very difficult to anticipate), we shall have exaggerated but unassailable manifestations of the feeling it has been sought to put down; and, while this is the employment of the *interim*, the party hit, who are by no means so closely tied to the alliance of the Church with the State, will, despairing of any other settlement, seek peace through its dissolution.

It may now perhaps in some degree appear why I

* Letter to Rev. Mr. Walker, pp. 23—26.

have pressed so earnestly the severance of these rubrical suits from "doctrinal significance." Could we but expel that noxious element from the debate, could we but see that the two conflicting views of the position and the vestments are just as capable, to say the least, of a large and innocuous as of a specific and contentious interpretation, then we might hope to see therewith a frame of mind among the litigators, capable of acquiescence in any judgment which they believe to be upright, and to be given after full consideration of the case. Soreness there might be, and murmuring; but good sense might prevail, and the mischief would be limited within narrow bounds. But unhappily men of no small account announce that they care not for the sign, they must deal with the thing signified. They desire the negation by authority of the doctrine of the Real Presence of our Lord and Saviour Christ, and of the Eucharistic Sacrifice; negations which, again, are synonymous with the disruption of the English Church.

When prudent men, or men made prudent by responsibility, are associated together for given purposes, whether in a cabinet, or a synod, or a committee, or a board, and they find their union menaced by differences of opinion, they are wont first to test very fully the minds of one another by argument and persuasion. Failing these instruments, both the instinct of self-preservation and the laws of duty combine in prompting them to put off the evil day, and thus to take the benefit of enlarged information, of fresh experience, of the softening influences of association, and of whatever other facilities of solution the unrevealed future may embrace. Why can we not carry a little of this forbearance, founded upon common sense, into religion, and at least fetch our controversies out of the torrid into the temperate zone?

The time may, and I hope will, arrive, when a spirit of more diffusive charity, a wider acquaintance with the language and history of Christian dogma, and a less jealous temper of self-assertion, will enable us to perceive how much of what divides us in the Eucharistic controversy is no better and no worse than logomachy, and how capable men, ridding themselves of the subtleties of the schools and eschewing heated reactions, may solve what passion and faction have often declared insoluble.

But that time has not yet arrived; and, if the doctrine of the Eucharist must really be recast, there are no alternatives before us except on the one hand disruption, on the other postponement of the issue until we can approach it under happier auspices. The auspices are not happy now. There are even those in the English Church who urge with sincerity, and without being questioned by authority, the duty of preaching the "Real Absence,"* and, though these be few, yet some who shrink from the word may be nearly with them in the thing. On the other side, wholly apart from the energy of partisanship, from a Romanizing disposition, and from a desire for the exaltation of an order, there are multitudes of men who can patiently endure differences which they believe to be provisional, and adjourn their settlement to a future day; but who believe that the lowering of the sacramental doctrine of the English Church, in any of its parts, will involve, together with a real mutilation of Scriptural and Catholic truth, a loss of her Christian dignity, and a forfeiture of all the hopes associated with her special position in Christendom. Of all sacramental doctrine, none is so tender in this respect as that which relates to the Eucharist. The gross abuses of practice, and the fanciful excesses of theological speculation in the Western Church before the Reformation, compelled the Anglican Reformers to retrench their statements to a minimum, which can bear no reduction, whether in the shape of altered formulæ, or of binding constructions. If, in these times of heat, we abandon the wise self-restraint which in the

* Rev. Mr. Wolfe on the "Eastward Position," p. 4.

main has up to a recent time prevailed, it is too probable that wanton tongues, prompted by ill-trained minds, may reciprocally launch their reproaches of superstition and idolatry on the one hand, of heresy and unbelief on the other. Surely prudence would dictate that in these circumstances all existing latitude of law or well-established practice should as a rule be respected; that no conscience be pressed by new theological tests, either of word or action; and that we should prefer the hope of a peaceful understanding, in some even distant future, to the certainty of a ruinous discord as the fruit of precipitancy and violent courses. One of the strangest freaks of human inconsistency I have ever witnessed is certainly this. We are much (and justly) reminded, with reference to those beyond our pale, to think little of our differences and much of our agreements; but at the same time, and often from the same quarters, we are taught and tempted by example if not by precept, within our own immediate "household of faith," to think incessantly of our differences, and not at all of our much more substantial and weighty agreements.

The proposition, then, on which I desire to dwell as the capital and cardinal point of the case is, that heavy will be the blame to those, be they who they may, who may at this juncture endeavour, whether by legislation or by judicial action, and whether by alteration of phrases or by needlessly attaching doctrinal significance to the injunction or prohibition of ceremonial acts, to shift the balance of doctrinal expression in the Church of England. The several sections of Christendom are teeming with lessons of all kinds. Let us, at least in this cardinal matter of doctrinal expression, wait and learn. We have received from the Almighty, within the last half-century, such gifts as perhaps were hardly ever bestowed within the same time on a religious community. We see a transformed clergy, a laity less cold and neglectful, education vigorously pushed, human want and sorrow zealously cared for, sin less feebly rebuked, worship restored from frequent scandal and prevailing apathy to uniform decency and frequent reverence, preaching restored to an Evangelical tone and standard, the organization of the Church extended throughout the Empire, and this by the agency, in many cases that might be named, of men who have indeed succeeded the Apostles not less in character than in commission. If we are to fall to pieces in the face of such experiences, it will be hard to award the palm between our infatuation and our ingratitude; and our just reward will be ridicule from without our borders, and remorse from within our hearts.

This highly-coloured description I desire to apply within the limits only of the definite statement with which it was introduced. But I am far from complaining of those who think the evils of litigation ought to be encountered, rather than permit even a handful of men to introduce into our services evidences of a design to Romanize the religion of the country. I have always, too, been of opinion that effective provision should be made to check sudden and arbitrary innovation as such, even when it does not present features of intrinsic mischief. To me this still appears a wiser and safer basis of proceeding than an attempt to establish a cast-iron rule of uniform obedience to a vast multitude of provisions sometimes obscure, sometimes obsolete, and very variously understood, interpreted, and applied. But this preference is not expressed in the interest of any particular party, least of all of what is termed the High Church party. For the rubrics, which the Public Worship Act is to enforce, may, with truth, be generally described as High Church rubrics; and the mere party man, who takes to himself that designation, has reason to be grateful to the opposing party for having so zealously promoted the passing of the Act. For my own part, I disclaim all satisfaction in such a compulsory enforcement of rubrics that I approve;

and I would far rather trust to the growth of a willing obedience among those who are called Low Churchmen, where it is still deficient. I am far, however, from asserting that all enforcement of the law, beyond what I have above described, must of necessity produce acute and fatal mischiefs. Much folly both of "reges" and of "Achivi" has been borne, and may yet be borne, if only Judgments shall be such as to carry on their front the note of impartiality, and so long as we avoid the rock of doctrinal significance, and maintain the integrity of the Prayer-Book.

But I must endeavour, before closing these remarks, to bring into view some further reasons against free and large resort to penal proceedings in regard to the ceremonial of the Church. The remarks I have to offer are critical in their nature, for they aim at exhibiting the necessary imperfections even of the best tribunal; but they do not require the sinister aid either of bitterness or of disrespect.

The first of these remarks is, that the extinction of the separate profession of the civilian, now merged in the general study and practice of the bar, and the consolidation of the Courts of Probate and Admiralty with those of Equity and Common Law, have materially impaired the chances, which have hitherto existed, of not finding in our Judges of ecclesiastical causes the form of fitness growing out of special study. Any reader of the learned Judgments of the Dean of Arches may perceive the great advantages they derive from this source. It may be thought, with some reason, that episcopal assessors will, in doctrinal cases, help to supply the defect; but it would not be easy to arrange that the most learned Bishops should be chosen as assessors; and the general standard of learning on the bench cannot, under the hard conditions of modern times, be kept very high. The number of individuals must at all times be small, who can unite anything like deep or varied learning with the administrative and pastoral qualities, and the great powers of business and active work, which are now more than ever necessary, and are almost invariably found, in a Bishop. But in questions of ceremonial, the difficulties are greater still.

Let any one turn, for example, to the decision on appeal in the Purchas case, as it is the most recent, and seems to be the most contested, of the rubrical decisions. He will find, perhaps with surprise, that it does not rest mainly on considerations of law, but much more upon the results of historical and antiquarian study. Though rightly termed a legal Judgment, and though it of course has plenary authority as to the immediate question it decides, it is in truth, and could not but be, as to the determining and main portion of it, neither more nor less than a purely literary labour. Now, the authority of literary inquiries depends on care, comprehensiveness, and precision, in collecting facts, and on great caution in concluding from them. There is no democracy so levelling as the Republic of Letters. Liberty and equality here are absolute, though fraternity may be sometimes absent on a holiday. And a literary labour, be it critical, be it technical, be it archæological, when it has done its immediate duty of disposing of a cause, cannot afterwards pass muster by being wrapped in the folds of the judicial ermine. It must come out into the light, and be turned round and round, just as freely (though under more stringent obligations of respect) as Professor Max Müller's doctrine of solar myths, or Professor Sylvester's fourth dimension in space, or Dr. Schliemann's promising theory that Hissarlik is Troy. It is, I believe, customary, and perhaps wise, that a prior judgment of the highest court of appeal should govern a later one. It is alleged, nor is it for me to rebut the allegation, that the Purchas Judgment contradicts the Judgment in the case of Liddell *v.* Westerton; but, if so, this is accidental, and does not touch the principle, which seems to be generally acknowledged. Now, however well this may stand with respect to interpretation of law, yet with respect to historical and antiquarian researches, and to Judgments which turn on them, it would evidently be untenable, and even ludicrous. And then comes the question, what right have we to expect from our Judges, amidst the hurry and pressure of their days, and often at a time of life when energy must begin to flag, either the mental habits, or the acquisitions, of the archæologist, the critic, or above all of the historian? Why should we expect of the Bishop, because he may be assumed to have a fair store of theology, or of the Judge, because he has spent his life in pleading or even in hearing causes, that they should be adepts in historical research, or that they should be imbued with that which is so rare in this country, the historic sense and spirit, abundant, in this our day, nowhere but in Germany?

It may be said that Judges can and will avail themselves of the labours of others; but they are unhappily not in the ordinary condition of courts of first instance, who can collect evidence of all kinds at will. They are confined to published labours, when they go beyond the *ex parte* statements with which counsel may supply them. Still, they are sure to do their best; and they may get on well enough, if the subject happens to be one of those which have been thoroughly examined, and where positive conclusions have been sufficiently established. But what if, on the contrary, it has been one neglected for many generations? if the authorities, so far as they go, are in serious if not hopeless conflict? if the study of the matter has but recently begun, and that only amidst the din and heat, and for the purposes, of the actual controversy? What is the condition of a Judge who has to interpret the law by means of *data*, which only the historian and the antiquarian can supply and digest respectively, when those valuable labourers have not digested or supplied them? For example, what if he have to investigate the question how a surplice is related to an alb, how far the use of either accompanies or excludes the cope or the chasuble (as a coat excludes a lady's gown), or in what degree the altar-wise position of the Holy Table had been established at the time when the Commissioners at the Savoy were engaged in the revision of the Liturgy? In this country a barrister cannot be his own attorney; yet a judge may not only have to digest his own legal apparatus, but may also be required to dive, at a moment's notice, into the *tohubohu* of inquiries, which have never yet emerged from the stage of chaos; and the decision of matters of great pith and moment for Christian worship and the peace of the Church comes to depend upon what is at best, by no fault of his, random and fragmentary knowledge.

Any reader of the Purchas Judgment on Appeal will perceive how truly I have said that it rests mainly, not on judicial interpretations, but on the results of literary research. In such interpretations, indeed, it is not wanting; but they are portions only of the fabric, and are joined together by what seems plainly to be literary and antiquarian inquiry. The Judicial Committee decide, for example, with regard to sacerdotal vestments, that the Advertisements of 1564 have the authority of law; and to this decision the mere layman must respectfully bow.* But they also rule that the Advertisements in prescribing the use of the surplice for parish churches, proscribe the use of the cope or the chasuble, and that the canons of 1603-4 repeat the prohibition.† Now, this is a proposition purely antiquarian. It depends upon a precise knowledge of the usages of what is sometimes termed "ecclesiastical millinery." Can Judges, or even Bishops, be expected to possess this very special kind of know-

* Brooke's Reports, pp. 171, 176.
† *Ibid.* p. 178. "If the minister is ordered to wear a surplice at all times of his ministration, he cannot wear an alb and tunicle when assisting at the Holy Communion; *if he is to celebrate the Holy Communion in a chasuble, he cannot celebrate in a surplice.*

ledge, or be held blameable for not possessing it? I think not. But when even Judges of great eminence, of the highest station, and of the loftiest character, holding themselves compelled to decide, aye or no, on the best evidence they can get, as to every question brought before them, proceed to determine that the use of the surplice excludes the use of the chasuble, this is after all a strictly literary conclusion, and is open to be confirmed, impaired, or overthrown, by new or widened evidence such as further literary labour may accumulate. And, indeed, it appears rather difficult to sustain the proposition that the surplice when used excludes all the more elaborate vestments, since we find it actually prescribed in one of the rubrics at the end of the Communion Office in the Prayer-Book of 1549, that the officiating minister is ordered to "*put upon him a plain alb or surplice with a cope.*"

Again, the Judicial Committee, in construing the rubrics as to the position of the minister, states that before the revision of 1662, " the custom of placing the table along the east wall was becoming general, and it may fairly be said that the revisers must have had this in view." This, of course, is a pure matter of history. Before and since the judgment was given, it has been examined by a variety of competent writers; and I gather from their productions, that had these been before the tribunal in 1871, it must have arrived, on this point, at an opposite opinion. The conclusion of Mr. Scudamore, indeed, is that the present position of the altars is the work of the eighteenth century.

The literary conclusion with respect to the surplice appears to be the foundation-stone of the Purchas judgment with reference to vestments. But it seems to be also collaterally sustained by three other propositions: one of which is, that the articles of visitation, and the proceedings of Commissions, in and after the reign of Elizabeth, prescribe the destruction of vestments, albs, tunicles, and other articles, as monuments of superstition and idolatry; the second, that the requisitions of Bishops in these parochial articles are limited to the surplice; the third, that there is no evidence of the use of vestments during the period. Now each and all of these are matters, not of law, but of historical criticism.

The critics of the Judgment are numerous; and few of them, perhaps, make due allowance for the difficulties under which it was framed. Their arguments are manifold, and far beyond my power fully to cite. Among other points, they admit the second of these three propositions, and consider that the attempts of the ruling authorities were limited, as regards enforcement, to the surplice; but hold that in those times what the law prescribed was one thing—what it enforced, or attempted to enforce, was another. Mr. MacColl* cites a remarkable example; namely, that while the Rubric required the priest to read daily four chapters of Holy Scripture, the Advertisements aimed at enforcing only two. The orders of destruction raise a point of great importance, which demands full inquiry. As far as I have noticed, they seem uniformly to include "crosses" as "monuments of superstition and idolatry;" yet the Judicial Committee in Westerton *v.* Liddell, and in Hebert *v.* Purchas, both decide that crosses for decoration of the building are lawful. As regards the actual use of vestments, Mr. MacColl (while presuming that in a penal case it is evidence of disuse, not of use, that is demanded) supplies what he thinks ample proof;† and it is noticed that in the judgment itself there is evidence, viz., that of Dering (1593), and Johnson (1573), sufficient to impede an universal assertion. But into these matters I do not enter. There is much more to be said upon them. My purpose is not one of controversy. I confine myself to urging the necessity of further historical and archæological inquiries, as absolutely necessary in order to

* "Lawlessness, Sacerdotalism, and Ritualism," p. 76.
† *Ibid.*, pp. 59—70.

warrant any judgments restrictive, in whatever sense, of the apparent liberality of our laws and practice; and I rejoice to see that for this end so many persons of ability, beside those I have named, are bringing in their respective contributions.*

I suppose it to be beyond doubt that in our times the acts of the officers of the law may be taken as evidence of what the law is, or is reported to be. The burning of printed editions of English books by the Customs would prove that the importation of such works was prohibited. But history seems to show that this apparently obvious rule cannot be applied to times like those of the Reformation without much caution and reserve. For example. The Purchas Judgment states that the law required the use of copes in cathedral and collegiate churches, and generally treats authorized destruction as evidence of illegality; but it appears† that the Queen's Commissioners at Oxford, in 1573 (when the anti-papal tide was running very high), ordered in the College Chapel of All Souls that all copes should be defaced and rendered unfit for use.

There are three cautionary remarks, with which I shall conclude.

* For example, Mr. Beresford Hope and Mr. Morton Shaw. Mr. Droop has produced some useful illustrations, unhappily not well arranged.

† Droop on Edwardian Vestments, p. 26.

The first is that, unless I am mistaken, the word evidence is sometimes used, in judgments on ceremonial, in a mode which involves a dangerous fallacy. It seems to be used in a judicial sense, whereas it is really used in a literary sense. As respects the testimony given in a case, the Judge deals judicially, and with his full authority as a Judge; but the illustrative matter he collects in these suits from books or pamphlets, laborious as he may be, and useful as it may be, is not evidence except in the sense in which Dr. Schliemann thinks he has plenty of evidence as to the site of Troy; it is historical inquiry, or literary or learned speculation.

The second is that, if I am right in laying down as the grand requisite for arriving at truth in these cases the historian's attainments and frame of mind, the Judge, and the lawyer, labour in these cases under some peculiar difficulties. It is almost a necessity for the Judge, as it is absolutely for the advocate, that every cause be resolved categorically by an Aye or a No. But the historical inquirer is not conversant with Aye and No alone: he is familiar with a thousand shades of colour and of light between them. The very first requisite of the historic mind is suspense of judgment. Judicial business requires, as a rule, a decision between two—it is the judgment of Solomon; but the historian may have to mince the subject into many fragments, according to the probabilities of the case; he deals habitually with conjectures and likelihoods, as well as positive assertions. The Judge has to give all where he gives anything, and his mental habit forms itself accordingly; but the "I doubt" which was so much criticized in Lord Eldon, is among the most prominent characteristics of the philosophic and truth-loving historian.

Lastly; after the famous judgment Mr. Burke has passed upon the immense merits, and besetting dangers, of the legal mind, with direct relation to the character of Mr. Grenville, that great master proceeds to state that "Mr. Grenville thought better of the wisdom and power of human legislation than in truth it deserves."* Most eminently does this seem to me to be true, in observing the manner after which our judges sometimes deal with ancient laws. Such as the character and efficacy of law is now, such they are apt to assume it always must have been. It has not been their business to consider the enormous changes in the structure of society, on its toilsome way through the rolling ages, from a low to a high organization. The present efficiency of law presumes the full previous inquiry and consultation of the deliberate power, and the perfect strength of the executive. But that

* Speech on American Taxation. Works, vol. ii. p. 389.

strength depends on the magistracy, the police, the judiciary, the standing army; upon the intercommunication of men, of tidings, of ideas, by easy locomotion; upon a crowd of arrangements for the most part practically unknown to the loosely compacted structures of mediæval societies. The moral force, which abode in them, had little aid, for the purposes of the supreme power, except on the most pressing emergencies, from material force; partial approximations were then only possible, in cases where the modern provisions for instant and general obedience are nearly complete. The law of to-day is the expression of a supreme will, which has, before deciding on its utterance, had ample means to consult, to scrutinize the matter, to adapt itself to practical possibilities; and it is justly construed as an instrument which is meant to take, and takes, immediate and uniform effect. But the laws of earlier times were to a great extent merely in the nature of authoritative assertions of principle, and tentative efforts towards giving it effect; and were frequently, not to say habitually, according to the expediencies of the hour, trampled under foot, even by those who were supposed to carry them into execution. Take the great case of Magna Charta, in which the community had so vast an interest. It was incessantly broken, to be incessantly, not renewed, but simply reaffirmed. And law was thus broken by authority, as authority found it convenient: from the age when Henry III. " passed his life in a series of perjuries," as is said by Mr. Hallam,* to the date when Charles II. plundered the bankers, Magna Charta was re-asserted, we are told, thirty-two times, without having been once repealed. But we do not therefore, from discovering either occasional or even wholesale disobedience, find it necessary to read it otherwise than in its natural sense. The reign of Elizabeth bisects the period between Magna Charta and ourselves. But very little progress had been made in her times towards improving the material order of society; and, from religious convulsion, they were in truth semi-revolutionary times. Acceding to the throne, she had to struggle with an intense dualism of feeling, which it was her arduous task to mould into an unity. The clergy, except a handful, sympathized largely with the old order, and continued very much in the old groove throughout the rural and less advanced districts. To facilitate her operations on this side, she wisely brought in the Rubric of Ornaments. But there had also sprung up in the kingdom, after the sad experience of Mary's reign, a determined Puritanism, lodged principally at the main centres of population, and sustained by the

---

* Middle Ages, ii. 451-3.

credit of the returning exiles (several of them Bishops), and by the natural sympathies of the Continental Reformation. Where this spirit was dominant, the work of destruction did not wait for authority, and far outran it. In truth, the powers of the Queen and the law were narrowly hedged in, on this side as well as on the other. What could be more congenial to her mind and to her necessities, than that, for all this second section of her people, she should wink hard at neglect in a sore point like that of vestments, and that in proceeding to the Advertisements of 1564, though obliged to apply a stronger hand, she should confine herself to expressing what she thought absolute decency required, namely, the surplice, and leave the rubric and the older forms, to be held or modified according to the progressive action of opinion? Considering the violent divergencies with which she had to deal, would it not have been the ruin of her work if she had endeavoured to push to the extremes now sometimes supposed the idea of a present and immediate uniformity throughout the land? This I admit is speculation, on a subject not yet fully elucidated; but it is speculation which is not in conflict with the facts thus far known, and which requires no strain to be put upon the language of the law.

"England expects every man to do his duty;" and

this is an attempt at doing mine, not without a full measure of respect for those who are charged with a task now more than ever arduous in the declaration and enforcement of the Act of Uniformity. To lessen the chances of misapprehension, I sum up, in the following propositions, a paper which, though lengthened, must, I know, be dependent to a large extent upon liberal interpretation.

I. The Church of this great nation is worth preserving; and for that end much may well be borne.

II. In the existing state of minds, and of circumstances, preserved it cannot be, if we now shift its balance of doctrinal expression, be it by an alteration of the Prayer-Book (either way) in contested points, or be it by treating rubrical interpretations of the matters heretofore most sharply contested on the basis of "doctrinal significance."

III. The more we trust to moral forces, and the less to penal proceedings (which are to a considerable extent exclusive one of the other), the better for the Establishment, and even for the Church.

IV. If litigation is to be continued, and to remain within the bounds of safety, it is highly requisite that it should be confined to the repression of such proceedings as really imply unfaithfulness to the national religion.

V. In order that judicial decisions on ceremonial may habitually enjoy the large measure of authority, finality, and respect, which attaches in general to the sentences of our courts, it is requisite that they should have uniform regard to the rules and results of full historical investigation, and should, if possible, allow to stand over for the future matters insufficiently cleared, rather than decide them upon partial and fragmentary evidence.

[The *Quarterly Review* for July, 1875 (p. 288 n.) observes that I have "stated the difficulty of acquiring knowledge on these subjects," and have "also illustrated it." Three instances are given :—

1. In relating a proceeding of the year 1573, I have "elevated" a college chapel into a collegiate church. This the Reviewer shows to have been contrary to the law of 1573, by referring to the Canons of 1603, and to the Act of Uniformity of 1662, which draws the distinction clearly. No such distinction is drawn in the Act of Elizabeth, which says, "In any cathedral or parish church, or other place within this realm," etc. It has therefore to be considered whether, unless and until the law dealt with them separately, churches under the charge of a body of clergy were or were not collegiate churches. The Rubric of 1559, prescribing weekly communion in cathedral and collegiate churches, added the reason of the provision, "where be many priests and deacons": a description eminently applicable to colleges. This question, I presume, can hardly be decided by the Reviewer's very original method of referring to enactments made, one thirty and the other ninety years afterwards.

But it is a question of law, on which I can only guide myself by the opinions of others. And the Reviewer is wrong in saying that I stated the difficulty of "acquiring knowledge" on these subjects. My remarks refer entirely to historical and antiquarian knowledge, from which I have been careful to distinguish matters of law.

The Reviewer's second point is that I have quoted as accurate a statement of Mr. MacColl, that, as the Rubric required the Clergy to read four chapters of Holy Scripture daily, and the "Advertisements" two, we have here a case in which the statute prescribed a major amount of observance, but the subaltern or executive authority was content with a minor amount. The Reviewer holds that the provision of the Advertisements was cumulative; and that it was obligatory on the Clergy of England, under severe penalties, to read, in all, six chapters of the Bible daily. His proofs are (p. 253) that—

1. The two chapters are to be read "with good advisement to the increase of my knowledge."

2. That "the service appointed" was to be read clearly and audibly, "that all the people may hear and understand."

On this ground he dismisses the opinion contrary to his own as "a gross misrepresentation." I leave it to Mr. MacColl to develop and sustain his statements; but to me the contention of the Reviewer seems to border on the incredible; and the "gross misrepresentation" to be a reasonable construction, if we bear in mind, what the Reviewer forgets or omits, namely, that the rubrical obligation of the clergyman as such—not of the officiating "curate" merely, with whom he confounds the wider class—was to say daily the morning and evening prayers in public *or in private*.

His third allegation is: "It is admitted that surplice and cope are to be worn together in cathedrals." Admitted by whom? By him, perhaps, after he has been informed of a Rubric of 1549, which perhaps he had also omitted to observe. But I was remarking on the Purchas Judgment, and no such admission is contained in the Purchas Judgment. It says, "The Vestment or Cope, Alb, and Tunicale, were ordered by the First Prayer-Book of Edward VI. . . . . The Canons . . . . ordered the surplice *only* to be used in parish churches." (Brook's "Judgments," pp. 175-6.) The Canons say nothing (Canon 58) of the surplice *only*. But the Judges put in the word only. If the Reviewer is right, this was a reckless or fraudulent interpolation. But he is wrong, and why? Because they evidently believed the use of the surplice excluded the use of the other vestments. This they have declared in express terms (see note, p. 95) as to chasuble, alb, and tunicle: and from the words I have quoted, "the Vestment or Cope," it seems they were not aware of any distinction between cope and chasuble: as again they dwell upon "the determination to remove utterly . . . *all* the vestments now in question." This, I may add, they think was proved by the Lincoln MS. which Mr. Peacock has published. Evidently the Judges proceeded upon the report of some most ill-informed informant, and had not read—as how could they read?—the work itself. For Mr. Peacock's volume, which they cite to show the destruction of "all the vestments," refers to some hundred parishes only, and, in about a score of these, reports that the cope was still retained.

I am sorry to have detained the reader with this exposure of the errors of a Reviewer, who really has not the same excuse, as may be reasonably alleged on behalf of the Judges of Appeal, for the misapprehension and consequent misstatement of history; in a discussion very wearisome in itself, but on which unhappily great practical issues are made to depend by the error of one party or of both.]

www.ingramcontent.com/pod-product-compliance
Lightning Source LLC
Chambersburg PA
CBHW030405170426
43202CB00010B/1503